MANAGING FAIRNESS IN ORGANIZATIONS

MANAGING FAIRNESS IN ORGANIZATIONS

Constant D. Beugré

QUORUM BOOKS
Westport, Connecticut • London

Library of Congress Cataloging-in-Publication Data

Beugré, Constant D.
    Managing fairness in organizations / Constant D. Beugré.
        p.   cm.
    Includes bibliographical references and index.
    ISBN 1–56720–211–X (alk. paper)
        1. Organizational behavior—Moral and ethical aspects.
    2. Personnel management—Moral and ethical aspects.   3. Distributive
    justice.   I. Title.
    HD58.7.B486   1998
    658.3—dc21   98–6017

British Library Cataloguing in Publication Data is available.

Library of Congress Catalog Card Number: 98–6017
ISBN: 1–56720–211–X

First published in 1998

Quorum Books, 88 Post Road West, Westport, CT 06881
An imprint of Greenwood Publishing Group, Inc.

Printed in the United States of America

The paper used in this book complies with the
Permanent Paper Standard issued by the National
Information Standards Organization (Z39.48–1984).

10 9 8 7 6 5 4 3 2 1

Contents

Preface

Justice is a social phenomenon, and as such has received a great deal of research attention from social psychologists and organizational behavior scholars. However, it was not until recently that books on organizational justice (perceptions of fair treatment within organizations) have been published, recognizing the importance of justice (or fairness) in organizations. Although this book follows that tradition, it takes a microperspective of organizational justice; that is, justice occurring within an organization. It does not, however, overlook macroorganizational justice aspects, such as fairness and customer satisfaction, fairness and environmental protection, and fairness issues in a global economy. This book is both descriptive and prescriptive: first, it analyzes the different theories of organizational justice (chapters 1, 2, and 3), its determinants (chapters 4 and 5), as well as its consequences (chapter 6); and second, based on this knowledge, it prescribes ways of creating fair working environments (chapter 7).

This book is devoted to organizational behavior and industrial/organizational scholars as well as managers. Not only does it represent an analysis of current research on the topic, but it also gives practical orientations on how to create fair working environments. Although organizational justice is not a panacea for managers, it can help boost employee morale and cooperation. Perceptions of unfairness have been related to several negative reactions, such as employee theft, lack of commitment, lawsuits, and, recently, aggressive behaviors in the workplace. In contrary, perceptions of fair treatment have been related to attitudinal and behavioral outcomes, such as employee commitment, trust, and cooperation, that are conducive to organizational performance.

This endeavor would not have been accomplished without the help of several people whom I would like to thank here. First, my former doctoral dissertation advisor, Professor Robert A. Baron, deserves special thanks. His comments and suggestions have considerably improved this work. I am grateful to my family for helping me both socially and emotionally as I worked in isolation for many long hours. As a Fulbright scholar at the Rensselaer Polytechnic Institute from 1993 to 1996, I used part of this scholarship to spend the spring semester of 1996 at Harvard University where I continued my work on the present book. I am grateful to my sponsor, the Institute of International Education in New York City and the United States Information Agency in Washington, D.C. All shortcomings of this book are mine.

Introduction

Studying organizational justice is important for at least three reasons: (1) justice is a social phenomenon and pervades every life, social or organizational; (2) the most important asset of any organization is its workforce —the manner in which it is treated influences subsequent attitudes and behaviors, such as commitment, trust, performance, turnover, aggression; and (3) we are moving toward a more educated workforce. As people become more skilled and educated, they request not only better jobs but also treatment with respect and dignity in the workplace. Greenberg (1987a; 426) notes that "we are entering an era in which issues of justice and fairness in many diverse forms will rise to the top of organizational behavior's collective research agenda." Similarly, Ulrich (1998, 124) contends that "the competitive forces that managers face today and will continue to confront in the future demand organizational excellence. The efforts to achieve such excellence through a focus on learning, quality, teamwork, and reengineering are driven by the way organizations get things done and how they treat their people." It is therefore important to understand justice issues in modern organizations.

DEFINITION OF ORGANIZATIONAL JUSTICE

The term organizational justice was first coined by Greenberg (1987a), referring to perceptions of fairness within organizations. According to Berg and Mussen (1975), the meaning of justice varies not only among individuals, but also among cultures, civilizations, and historical eras. The authors consider justice synonymous to fairness. Rawls (1971, 3) also refers to justice as fairness. He pointed out that "justice is the first virtue of social institutions as truth is of systems of thought." But what is justice? And what is fairness? The first two definitions imply that justice is that which has been considered fair by members of a given society or group. Justice is a complex phenomenon and as suggested by Reis (1984, 38), "the problem for both lay person and researchers originate in the definition of justice: Just what is just?" The author, however, did not suggest a clear definition of justice. Sheppard, Lewicki, and Minton (1992) have suggested a definition of justice more fitted to organizational settings, which refers to two principles. The first principle of justice requires a judgment of *balance* (comparison of two similar actions in similar situations) and the second principle, correctness, refers to a quality which makes the decision seem right.

The concept of balance as described by the authors is close to that of equity (Adams, 1963, 1965). The principle of balance is applied when one compares an outcome received to that of another person, or to his or her own contributions. If the outcomes and the inputs fit, the person will certainly feel a sense of balance, implying justice. However, a discrepancy will lead to a perception of injustice. According to Sheppard, Lewicki, and Minton (1992, 10), "comparisons of balance are made by evaluating the outcomes of two or more people and equating those outcomes to the value of the inputs they provided." Also according to the authors, correctness refers to the "quality that makes the decision seem 'right,' the determination of which encompasses aspects of consistency, accuracy, clarity, procedural thoroughness, and compatibility with the morals and values of the times." One decides about the "perceived justice of some action that harms or benefits someone by deciding whether the action appears to be both balanced and correct. If it appears to be both balanced and correct, then it is judged to be fair. If it is neither, then it is deemed to be unfair" (12).

"Organizational justice refers to the perceived fairness of the distribution of outcomes and procedures used to make these distributions"

(Citera and Rentsch, 1993, 211). Organizational justice is also defined as individuals' and groups' perceptions of the fairness of treatment (including, but not limited to, allocations) received from organizations, and their behavioral reactions to such perceptions (James, 1993). Although allowing a better understanding of fairness in organizations, these definitions are somehow restrictive and seem limited to the two popular dimensions of organizational justice: distributive justice and procedural justice. They ignore other dimensions of organizational justice, such as interactional justice and systemic justice. For Bies and Tripp (1995), justice in organizations refers to the rules and social norms in organizations governing: (1) how outcomes should be allocated; (2) the procedures that should be used to make decisions; and (3) how people should be treated interpersonally. This definition implies the existence of three dimensions of organizational justice: distributive justice, procedural justice, and interactional justice.

Building on Bies and Tripp's conceptualization of organizational justice, I suggest a broader definition: *Organizational justice refers to the perceived fairness of the exchanges taking place in an organization, be they social or economic, and involving the individual in his or her relations with superiors, subordinates, peers, and the organization as a social system.* This definition implies that justice issues may be considered in relation to the interactions with other individuals (interactional justice), to the organization as a social system (systemic justice), and to the fairness of the rewards received (distributive justice) and the formal procedures and methods (procedural justice). Like previous definitions (e.g., Berg and Mussen, 1975; Rawls, 1971), this definition also considers justice as fairness. Therefore, in this book, the terms "justice" and "fairness" will be used interchangeably. Organizational justice scholars (e.g., Greenberg, 1987a, 1990a; Folger, 1977; Sheppard, Lewicki, and Minton, 1992, Cropanzano, 1993) have used these terms interchangeably. However, one must notice that the term "justice" has a legal connotation and seems broader than the concept of fairness, which seems more limited. But to remain in the tradition of organizational justice scholars, the two terms are here considered synonymous.

JUSTICE AS A PERCEPTUAL PHENOMENON

According to Bazerman (1993), justice is fundamentally a perceptual phenomenon; it is not an objective state, but a judgment. The author argues further that fairness is a perception: "We are all entitled to our judgments about what we think is fair" (189). As Furby (1986) puts it, perceived justice is an evaluative judgment about the rightness of a person's fate or treatment by others. Sheppard, Lewicki, and Minton (1992) contend that what is important is not reality itself, but the perceptions of reality: "A critical point in all such judgments is perceptions. For all interests and purposes, reality is not consequential, so differences between perceptions and reality are not relevant. We act on our own perceptions, and must deal with the perceptions of the people with whom we interact" (12). There is no absolute standard for deciding fairness in a given situation. Judgments of fairness are always relative. They are influenced by several factors, including the situation itself, the individual's group membership, and his or her tolerance to ambiguous stimuli. What is fair for an individual X may be unfair to an individual Y. The authors contend that justice judgments are always relative, influenced by one's social motivation or philosophy, and one's own group membership. As beauty lies in the eye of the beholder, justice lies in the eye of the perceiver (Sheppard, Lewicki, and Minton, 1992; Saal and Moore, 1993).

The essence of justice is perceptual. "What is actually just by some objective and independent standard, really matters a lot less than what is perceived to be just" (Sheppard, Lewicki, and Minton, 1992, p. 9). Therefore, an organizational setting that employee A perceives as being just may be perceived as unjust by employee B. Despite this perceptual and subjective aspect of justice, it is possible to suggest a minimum standard of justice. Being treated with respect and dignity may be perceived as just by most people. For instance, an employee's perceptions of criticism emanating from his or her supervisor influences his or her own reactions. Baron (1993) suggests that when criticism is perceived as fair, the information it contains is subjected to careful scrutiny and elaborate processing. In contrast, when criticism is perceived as being unfair or unjustified, relatively little processing of the information follows.

Greenberg (1990c) also recognized the perceptual nature of justice. If justice is perceptual, then, organizational justice is no more than impression management. Impression management refers to the conscious or unconscious attempt to control images that are projected in real or imagined social interactions (Schlenker, 1980). "Injustice (or justice) is a perception, not an objective fact. It lies in the eye of the beholder and cannot, by its very nature, be accurately inferred from any measures of objective outcomes" (Martin and Murray, 1984, p. 110). Agreement of two or more persons on the perception of justice is improbable (Adams and Freedman, 1976). The subjectivity of justice raises the issue of its study in organizations. Why do we study organizational justice? Who determines the fairness of a particular action? Why do people pursue justice at all? Answers to these questions are related to the importance of justice, not only as a social phenomenon, but also as a topic of investigation and a human virtue.

SOCIALIZATION AND FORMATION OF JUSTICE PERCEPTIONS

How do people form perceptions or standards of justice? Socialization plays an important role in this process. Tyler (1987) notes that the development of procedural justice is part of the general socialization process, similar to political socialization. According to Lerner (1987, 59):

just as Americans learn that democracy is a good form of government, they also learn that the adversary process is the fair way to resolve disputes. This socialization might occur in childhood, when basic political and social predispositions are formed, or it might occur later in the ongoing socialization process that involves cultural institutions, such as the mass media. The socialization process suggests that cultural norms about fairness should generally correspond with citizens' views about what is fair.

Group membership in some cultures may influence perceptions of justice. People tend to perceive in-group members more favorably than out-group members. Awareness of in-group/out-group distinctions and intergroup competition can lessen concerns with applying justice rules equally to all individuals (Deutsch, 1985; Kramer, 1991; Tajfel and Turner, 1979). Deutsch (1985) distinguished two types of justice related to in-group and out-group: *inclusionary* and *exclusionary* justice. Justice becomes exclusionary when individuals apply justice principles only to members of the in-group and inclusionary when justice principles and procedures are seen as universally applicable. In collectivist cultures, people are more likely to pursue conflicts with out-group members (Triandis, 1989), thereby using an exclusionary justice approach. Individualistic cultures promote equity approaches to allocations, whereas collectivist cultures and value systems promote equality or need allocations (Deutsch, 1975; Hasegawara, 1986; Triandis, 1989).

Mann, Radford, and Kanagawa (1985) conducted an experimental study on a sample of Japanese and Australian children. They found that Japanese children used decision rules that provided the majority and minority with an equal opportunity to obtain rewards, whereas Australian children used decision rules that favored self-interest. Children in collectivist cultures may be socialized to favor group harmony, whereas children in individualist cultures may be socialized to seek self-interest.

Deutsch (1985, 59) introduced the concept of *scope of justice* which refers to the extent to which people include others in their moral community. For Deutsch, an individual tolerates injustice by excluding the "victim from his or her definition of the community in which his or her moral standards are applied." People are more apt to believe that principles of fairness apply to social entities who are included in, rather than excluded from, their moral community (Brockner, 1994). An important element in defining the moral community is psychological attachment. An individual may tolerate an injustice from someone to whom he or she is psychologically attached more than from someone with whom such attachment does not exist. In organizational settings, a subordinate may well tolerate an injustice coming from a supervisor with whom the employee has close ties than from a distant colleague or supervisor. The next section focuses on the importance of pursuing fairness in organizations.

OBJECTIVES FOR PURSUING JUSTICE

Pursuing justice may be an end in itself, but also a means for further actions. Fairness is a desired social state and people seek to present themselves as fair to themselves and to others (Greenberg, 1990c). Sheppard, Lewicki, and Minton (1992) identified three reasons why people strive for justice—performance effectiveness, sense of community, and individual dignity and humanness:

1. Performance effectiveness. Fairness considerations may enhance positive attitudes in employees and thereby positively influence their performance. In this sense, justice reflects a concern for achievement (Deutsch, 1985). This refers to an instrumental approach of justice. Justice is a means to an end.

2. Being just also ensures a sense of community. Deutsch (1985) considered cooperation enhancement as a purpose of being fair. Fairness increases the sense of identification and membership within an organization. "The individual tries to achieve a sense of membership in, and identification with, some social entity: a work unit, department, division, or organization" (Sheppard, Lewicki, and Minton, 1992, 18).

3. Finally, justice ensures a sense of individual dignity and humanness. Treating another person fairly implies that he or she is respected, considered as a human being. Sheppard Lewicki, and Minton (1992) suggest that outcomes, procedures, and systems should operate in a manner that preserves a sense of well-being, individual identity, and personal worth. Here, justice is an end in itself.

These three objectives for pursuing justice may help improve interpersonal relations among organizational members and develop positive attitudes toward the organization as well. The pursuit of justice prevents an organization from incurring the costs associated with lack of justice and due process. It also enhances the legitimacy of the system or the decision. According to Sheppard, Lewicki, and Minton (1992, 103), "perceptions of justice lead to perceptions of perceived legitimacy, which in turn lead to compliance with the system." The authors suggest that the serious pursuit of justice also serves organizational efficiency and effectiveness. Justice is not an end in itself, but a means to attain more desired goals. People's attitudes about justice follow an instrumental strategy. "When it is advantageous to behave fairly, people will do so. Presumably, when it is not advantageous, people will act in a manner inconsistent with existing norms" (Reis, 1984, 35). This instrumental strategy is also recognized by Deutsch (1975, 140) who suggests that the "natural values of justice are thus the values which foster effective social cooperation to promote individual well-being. It is this conception which is dominant in most theories of organizational justice." For instance, understanding fairness is important because "the way people are treated in organizations exerts a powerful effect on their reactions that is independent of the objective features of the work environment" (Aquino, Griffeth, Allen, and Hom, 1997, 1222).

This book is divided into seven chapters: the first three discuss theories of distributive justice, procedural justice, and interactional justice; chapter 4 analyzes individual characteristics influencing justice perceptions; chapter 5 focuses on the role of organizational factors in shaping people's perceptions of justice; chapter 6 analyzes employee reactions to perceived justice (or injustice); and finally, chapter 7 suggests ways of creating fair working environments.

Distributive Justice

This chapter discusses current theories of distributive justice. These theories include: equity theory (Adams, 1965; Walster, Walster, and Berscheid, 1978), Deutsch's theory of distributive justice (Deutsch, 1985), justice motive theory (Lerner, 1975, 1981), Jasso's theory of distributive justice (Jasso, 1977, 1978), and relative deprivation theory (Crosby, 1976, 1982, 1984). Early studies of justice focused on the concept of distributive justice, a term first introduced by Homans (1961). Distributive justice refers to the perceived fairness of the distribution of outcomes, and distributive justice theory has served as the basis for the development of equity theory and subsequent models of distributive justice (Deutsch, 1985).

EQUITY THEORY

Equity theory deals with the distribution of outcomes in an exchange relationship involving at least two people. In the following sections, I analyze the main theories of equity (Adams, 1963, 1965; Walster, Walster, and Berscheid, 1978). Since these two theories have been extensively discussed in the literature, I will only review their main components.

Adams's Theory of Equity

Equity theory (Adams, 1963, 1965) focuses on the reactions of a person when considering the ratio of his or her inputs to that of a comparison other. Adams's theory was based on Homans's (1961) model of distributive justice. Homans identified what each person brings to the relationship as *investments* (or costs), and what he or she gets as *profits* or (rewards). The person compares the ratio of his or her investments/rewards to that of a comparison other. When the two ratios are equal, the person experiences a feeling of justice. However, any discrepancy between the two leads to a feeling of injustice.

Building on this reasoning, Adams (1965) contends that when a person's outputs are equal to his or her inputs, and the same situation prevails for the referent, there is a feeling of equity. However, when a discrepancy occurs between the two, the individual experiences feelings of inequity and engages in inequity-reduction behaviors. Interests for equity theory aroused in the sixties and seventies (e.g., Pritchard, 1969; Walster, Walster, and Berscheid, 1978). Such interest led Weick (1966, 439) to argue that:

> equity theory appears to be among the more useful middle-range theories of organizational behavior. It clearly has guided organizational researchers into problem areas that were unfamiliar but highly relevant, and it has generated experiments, the outcomes of which any responsible theorist must cope with. A theory that can produce such outcomes in such a short time warrants increased inputs from investigators.

Research on equity theory (Adams, 1963, 1965; Adams and Freedman, 1976; Walster, Walster, and Berscheid, 1978; Cowherd and Levine, 1992) has shown four ways of dealing with injustice: live with it, change the comparison other, change one's behavior to remove the injustice (rationalize the injustice by making a cognitive alteration of the situation), or leave the situation. Adams (1963, 1965) developed the following formula to describe equity theory:

$$\frac{I_{ind}}{Out_{ind}} > \frac{I_O}{Out_O} \quad \text{or} \quad \frac{O_A}{I_A} < \frac{O_B}{I_B}$$

where I_{ind} refers to the individual's input, Out_{ind} to his or her output, I_O refers to the comparison other's input, and Out_O to the comparison other's output. Input represents what the person brings to the relationship. Inputs may be effort, education, skills, age, and so forth. Outcome is what the person obtains as member of a relationship. In organizational settings, outcomes may include pay, promotion, demotion, benefits, and rewards. Inequity may also occur when the outputs are superior to the inputs.

Several studies on reactions to perceived inequity found that people lowered their performance when they were underpaid and raised it when they were overpaid (Adams and Freedman, 1976; Greenberg, 1982). Greenberg (1989) found that employees cognitively augmented the perceived importance of work environment features as contributors to their overall payment equity. They also tended to exaggerate the perceived level of these outcomes needed to establish equity. This reaction seems to be a "coping strategy," similar to what is suggested by cognitive dissonance theory (Festinger, 1954). To cope with a situation of underpayment, the individual tends to rationalize it by finding in the environment more positive incentives, thereby restoring equity.

Walster, Walster, and Berscheid's Theory of Equity

Four basic propositions characterize Walster, Walster, and Berscheid's equity theory:

1. Individuals will try to maximize their outcomes.

2. Groups can maximize collective reward by evolving accepted system for equitably apportioning rewards and costs among members.

3. When individuals find themselves participating in inequitable relationships, they become distressed. The more inequitable the relationship, the more distress the individual feels.

4. Individuals who discover that they are in an inequitable relationship attempt to eliminate their distress by restoring equity. The greater the inequity, the more distress they feel, and the harder they try to restore equity.

The authors developed a more complex formula of equity theory:

$$\frac{(O_A - I_A)}{(|I_A|)^{K_A}} = \frac{(O_B - I_B)}{(|I_B|)^{K_A}}$$

where A and B are the two people involved in a relationship.

O_A and O_B = A and B's outcomes

$|I_A|$ and $|I_B|$ = absolute values of A and B's inputs

The exponents k_A and k_B take on the value of +1 or −1, depending on whether the product of I times $(O_A - I_A)$ has a plus or minus sign.

K_A = sign (I_A) X sign $(O_A - I_A)$

K_B = sign (I_B) X sign $(O_B - I_B)$

Inputs may be assets or liabilities. The inputs that a participant contributes to a relationship can be either assets, which entitle him or her to rewards, or liabilities, which entitle him or her to suffer costs (Walster, Walster, and Berscheid, 1976, 1978). In this theory of equity, outcomes refer to positive as well as negative consequences of an exchange. A relationship is equitable when the two equations are equal. But how to translate these equations in real-life situations appears quite difficult, at least in terms of computation. Take the example of two employees (employee A and employee B) who are asked to work together on an assigned project. Suppose that their inputs are the time and effort each devotes to the project, and employee A devotes less time and effort than employee B. When completed, the project will yield $100,000 to the company. According to the company's internal policy and motivational system, employees who have worked on a project receive 10 percent of the benefits yielded. The two employees together receive $10,000, each getting $5,000. Suppose that employee A's time and effort are estimated at –2, while employee B's time and effort are estimated at +3. Both bonuses are estimated at +5 each. In applying Walster, Walster, and Berscheid's formula, the following numbers are obtained:

$I_A = -2$ and $O_A = +5$

$I_B = +3$ and $O_B = +5$

$K_A = (-) \times (+) = -$

$K_B = (+) \times (+) = +$

The result for employee A yields: $5-(-2)/(2)^{-1} = 7/1/2 = 14$.

For employee B, the result is $(5-3)/(3) = 2/3$.

These results show that this relationship is an inequitable one, since employee A is overrewarded compared to the time and effort devoted to the project, while employee B is underrewarded. Although previous investigations stated that under an overpayment situation, people tend to feel guilty (Homans, 1961; Adams, 1965), this is less obvious in real situations. In the present case, it is not obvious that employee A will feel guilty and attempt to give the money back. However, for employee B, the situation is quite an inequitable one, since the effort and time devoted to the project are not rewarded accordingly. For this situation to be equitable, one would expect employee A to get less than he or she received and employee B to get more than employee A. Additional computations consider that for the relationship to be equitable, employee B should get +45 and employee A +5, or employee A should get –1 and employee B +5.

Walster, Walster, and Berscheid (1978) identified two types of distress an advantaged person may feel in an inequitable relationship. The first is *retaliation distress*. An individual benefiting from an inequitable relationship may fear revenge from the other party. The second is *self-concept distress* (loss of self-esteem). In this case, the self-esteem of the person benefiting from the inequitable relationship may suffer. The authors labeled the benefactor of an inequitable relationship, the exploiter. Like Adams (1963, 1965), they recognized the role of perceptions in equity. What is equitable for a given individual may be perceived as inequitable by another. Despite its interests and several studies to validate its concepts, equity theory was criticized by several scholars.

Critique of Equity Theory

The incomplete nature of equity theory was underscored by Deutsch (1985, 25): "My objections to equity theory center not so much on its incompleteness, but rather on several other concerns: the nonstrategic characterization of the relationship between the parties in an exchange relationship; its motivational and cognitive assumptions; and the conception of justice that is implicit in the equity formulation." Despite this criticism, Deutsch recognizes the importance of equity theory. He contends that Adams's major contributions to the development of equity theory were to employ Festinger's (1954) theory of cognitive dissonance in characterizing the processes involved in reducing the tensions associated with perceived inequity and to initiate the experimental investigation of some of the implications of equity theory. Other studies (e.g., Lawler, 1968; Pritchard, 1969) found that procedures used to analyze the effects of equity (or inequity) were challenging participants' self-esteem or threatening their job security. Greenberg (1978) also notices that a psychological distance effect tends to influence feelings of inequity. Feelings of inequity are stronger when the overpayment disadvantages a comparison person who is liked more than one who is disliked.

The role of individual variables was also neglected in research on equity. As Miles, Hatfield, and Huseman (1994, 586) put it, "one problem with early equity research was its failure to incorporate individual differences in its predictions." Huseman, Hatfield, and Miles (1987) developed the concept of *Equity Sensitivity* to improve the predictability of equity theory and incorporate the role of individual differences. According to these authors, reactions to inequity depend on the sensitivity of the person. They identified three types of persons: *Equity Sensitives, Benevolents,* and *Entitleds.* An Equity Sensitive person views equity as a relation in which his or her own input/output ratio matches that of the comparison other. A Benevolent prefers that his or her input/output ratio be less than that of the comparison other. An Entitled, however, prefers relations where his or her input/output ratio is more than that of the comparison other. The authors considered equity sensitivity as a personality trait representing values emanating from both cultural and individual psychological areas. Changes in a person's preferences presumably would occur rarely and only as the consequences of grossly significant changes in the situation. Miles, Hatfield, and Huseman (1994) note that Benevolents better tolerate a situation of inequity than Entitleds and Equity Sensitives. The authors studied the attitudes of banking and public utility employees and found that pay was more important for Equity Sensitives and Entitleds, whereas sense of accomplishment was more important for Benevolents. They also found that Entitleds had a stronger preference for extrinsic, tangible outcomes than Benevolents and Equity Sensitives.

Berger, Zelditch, Anderson, and Cohen (1972) developed a status-value model of equity theory. They contend that an individual's reactions to inequity result not from comparisons to a specific other individual (local comparison), but from comparisons to a generalized other (referent comparison) such as an occupational group. Despite this addition to equity theory, these authors did not consider the importance of different rules in making justice judgments, unlike Leventhal (1976), who developed a justice judgment model of distributive justice.

THE JUSTICE JUDGMENT MODEL

Leventhal (1976, 1980) developed a justice judgment model of distributive justice based on previous works (Homans, 1961; Adams, 1965). The justice judgment model focuses on the conditions under which people proactively employ various justice norms (Greenberg and Leventhal, 1976). This theory suggests that the distributive system is a function of the goal sought by the participants in a relationship. Leventhal identifies several rules of distributive justice, the most important being the rule of equity, the rule of equality, and the rule of need. The author contends that when the goal is performance, equity is likely to be the justice norm, whereas equality is the justice norm when harmony is the preferred goal. It is also possible to distribute outcomes according to the needs of each recipient. An allocation norm is defined as a social rule which specifies criteria that define certain distributions of rewards and resources as fair and just. Leventhal (1976, 95) suggests that "an allocator's decision to comply with one allocation norm rather than another, represents not only an attempt to be fair and just, but also an attempt to gain the unique pattern of instrumental benefits that is associated with following that norm." He further contends that "in fact, it seems likely that an allocator who distributes rewards equitably frequently does so more because he desires to maximize long-term productivity than because he desires to comply with an abstract standard of justice. His decisions are based on an expectancy that equitable distributions of reward will elicit and sustain high levels of motivation and performance" (96).

Leventhal, Michaels, and Sanford (1972) found that subjects who desired to prevent interpersonal conflict increased the worst performer's share of reward at the expense of the best performer. Their results showed that reward allocation was also influenced by secrecy. Under secrecy, subjects were less likely to inflate the rewards of the worst performer. The authors concluded that secrecy about the distribution of reward reduces the allocator's fear of antagonism and conflict, and permits him or her to follow his or her own standard of equity more closely. However, when there is full disclosure of information about the distribution of reward, an allocator prefers a distribution which is likely to minimize dissatisfaction and antagonism among inferior performers.

In allocating outcomes, it is important to negotiate a compromise between productivity enhancement and harmony among employees. As suggested by Kabanoff (1991), organizations are both task and social systems that involve simultaneous pressures for economic performance and the maintenance of social cohesion. Kabanoff also suggests that power creates a fundamental justice dynamic. He further notes that equity principle is preferred when power differences are large among the allocator and the recipient (power is centralized), and equality is preferred when power differences are small (power is decentralized).

Leventhal (1976, 99) believes that the search for justice may be a means instead of an end in itself. He suggests an instrumental notion of justice: "An allocator can improve group productivity by using rewards to regulate group membership. Equitable distributions of reward make group membership more attractive for recipients who contribute more." According to the justice judgment model, an individual uses four stages to evaluate the fairness of outcomes:

1. the individual decides which justice rules are applicable and how much weight to accord to each;
2. the individual estimates the amount and type of outcome the recipient deserves based on each rule;
3. the individual combines the outcomes deserved on the basis of each rule into a final estimate; and
4. the individual evaluates the justice of the actual outcome by comparing the actual to the deserved outcome.

Leventhal, Karuza, and Fry (1980) developed the concept of distributive preferences, attitudes that predispose an individual to favor certain distributions over others. According to the authors, these distributive preferences are influenced by norms relative to the individual's educational, family, and economic background.

The justice judgment model is proactive, whereas equity theory is reactive. The justice judgment model intends to set the rules leading to fairness in a given situation. Equity is relevant when the goal of the allocator is toward enhancing economic productivity, equality rule is used when harmony among group members is sought, and need is preferred when the allocator intends to satisfy the needs of each member. Leventhal (1976) also added the concept of *reciprocal justice*, which refers to the intent of the individual to treat the other person as he or she was treated in the past. Martin and Harder (1987) have confirmed the existence of several justice rules in a laboratory setting. They found that individuals used contribution rules to distribute more financial rewards, and equality and need-based rules to distribute more socioe-motional rewards. However, one limitation of their study was that their subjects (undergraduate students) were role-playing in a labora-tory setting. These results may differ in a real-life situation; neverthe-less, they confirm previous findings which underscore the existence of several rules of justice (e.g., Deustch, 1985, Lerner, 1981; Leventhal, 1976, 1980).

DEUTSCH'S THEORY OF DISTRIBUTIVE JUSTICE

According to Deutsch (1985), distributive justice is concerned with the distribution of the conditions and goods that affect individual well-being, broadly defined to include its psychological, physiological, economic, and social aspects. Deutsch (1975, 1985) suggests that the distribution of goods (positive outcomes), as well as harms (negative outcomes), depends on seven elements:

1. *The nature of the good or harm being distributed.* Injustice may occur in considering the nature of the goods and harms dis-tributed. It may also occur in viewing the quality and quan-tity of the outcomes.

2. *The roles involved in the distribution process.* Injustice may oc-cur when the roles involved in the distribution process are not performed by appropriately qualified people.

3. *The styling and timing of the distribution.* The sense of injus-tice can be elicited or intensified by the timing of a distribu-tion of a social good or harm. This rule refers to the way the distribution principle is specified and the time lag between the action and the distribution of the outcome. If a reward is given long after an outstanding performance, the recipient may not perceive it as fair. In the same manner, if a punish-ment is administered long after a "crime" is committed, it may seem unfair. In addition, "a distribution process that is

shrouded in secrecy encourages the suspicion that the secrecy is hiding something that would argue dissent or disagreement if it were revealed; it stimulates doubts about the justice of the distribution as well as the justice of the procedures employed" (Deutsch, 1985, 33).

4. *The value underlying the distribution.* The value chosen by the allocator may be considered just or unjust. Suppose that a manager decides to introduce a performance-based compensation system. This system may be profitable to outstanding employees, whereas others less qualified or not willing to make extra efforts may perceive it as unjust.

5. *The rules or criteria employed to represent the values.* These rules and criteria may not be shared by all the parties involved in the exchange process.

6. *The measurement procedures used to implement the criteria.* "The sense of injustice may be aroused by the implementation of the accepted rules for defining the chosen distributive principle" (Deutsch, 1985, 34).

7. *The way decisions are made about any of the foregoing.* "Here, the injustice lies in the methods by which the decisions are made rather than in the substance of the decisions" (Deutsch, 1985, 34).

Deutsch's model of distributive justice also emphasizes an instrumental view of justice: "There is usually a positive, circular relation between individuals' well-being in a group and the well-functioning of that group. The more satisfied the individuals are, the better their group functions, and vice versa" (1985, 140). The "natural values of justice" are thus, according to Deutsch, the values which foster effective social cooperation to promote individual well-being. He shares with Leventhal the importance of using several rules of justice (equity, equality, and need). Deutsch also suggests that the distribution system under which a group functions can significantly affect interactions among its members. This effect is likely to be reduced "if the task or social context of the group has demand characteristics that are incongruent with the social relations induced by the distributive system" (162). Deutsch notes that an experienced injustice, whether to oneself or to another, involves one as a member of a "moral community" whose moral norms are being violated, and it evokes an obligation to restore justice. He also notices that the sensitivity to an injustice is greater among those who are disadvantaged than among those who are advantaged by it. Although his model focuses on the distribution of outcomes, Deutsch recognizes the importance of procedures, as does Lerner (1975, 1977) in his model of justice motive.

THE JUSTICE MOTIVE THEORY

According to the justice motive theory, the form of justice followed in making allocation decisions depends on the nature of the relations between the parties involved in conjunction with the focus of the parties on each other as individuals or as occupants of positions (Lerner, 1977). There is a direct relationship between a person's commitment to deserving his or her own outcomes (personal contract) and the extent to which others are able to receive the outcomes they deserve (Lerner, 1975; Rubin and Peplau, 1975). Lerner (1977) developed the concept of *belief in a just world* that influences justice evaluations. Ball, Trevino, and Sims (1993) analyze the effect of belief in a just world (BJW) on fairness judgments concerning punishments in organizations. They found that subordinates with a strong belief in a just world perceived punishments to be more procedurally than distributively fair. They also expressed more trust in and satisfaction with the supervisor, higher organizational commitment, and lower turnover intentions. In an empirical study, Steensma, Hartigh, and Lucardie (1994) found that the higher the belief in a just world, the less sympathy respondents felt for the victim of an occupational accident.

Lerner (1975, 1977) also identifies several distribution norms, including: the justice of needs, the justice of social obligations and contract, the justice of parity, the justice of equity, the Darwinian justice, and the justice of self-interest. Like Leventhal (1980) and Deutsch (1985), Lerner contends that the form of justice preferred depends on the goal of the individual. According to Lerner (1981, 22), "the most important step in developing an adequate theory of justice is to recognize that the traditional assumption that people are continually and centrally concerned with maximizing their outcomes must inevitably lead to a model that fails to capture the unique qualities associated with justice" (p. 22).

Lerner (1975) also developed the concept of *justice of entitlement*, which refers to justice occurring when an individual empathizes with the occupant of a position. "The individual is identified with someone, anyone, in that position" (Lerner, 1977, 42). Also important in this theory is the concept of deserving, which evolves at an early age when the child learns to delay immediate gratifications for further gratifications. According to Lerner (1977, 7), "a central tenet of justice theory is that the development of the commitment to deserving, the personal contract, appears as a natural consequence of human development." But unlike other models of distributive justice (Deutsch, 1985; Leventhal, 1976), the justice motive model takes into account the role of an observer in justice evaluations. Justice evaluations made by an observer depend mostly on his or her tendency to believe in a just world. According to Lerner, Miller, and Holmes (1976), the more one perceives one's partner as a unique individual rather than an anonymous occupant of a social role, the more salient equality is relative to equity. The importance of the observer is also noticed in Jasso's model of distributive justice.

JASSO'S THEORY OF DISTRIBUTIVE JUSTICE

Jasso (1977, 1978, 1980, 1983, 1994) developed a new model of distributive justice which is mathematically formulated as compared to others. For Jasso (1994), any scientific study of justice should focus on three questions:

1. What do individuals and collectivities think is just?
2. What is the magnitude of the injustice associated with specified departures from perfect justice?

3. What are the behavioral and social consequences of perceived injustice?

Answers to these questions have led to the development of a model of distributive justice which identifies three elements: just reward (JR), just reward function (JRF), and just reward distribution (JRD). Jasso (1983) defines *just reward* as the amount or level of a good which an observer considers to be just for an individual of particular characteristics. The *just reward function* is the rule that specifies the worth in just reward units of a set of characteristics. Just reward distribution is that frequency of distribution of a good in a population which is considered by an observer to be just; it has a specified distribution form and parameters, such as a minimum income or a particular amount of dispersion. An important element of this theory is the role of the observer who may be the rewardee, a specific individual, or a social entity. Jasso's theory implies the existence of an internal standard (which is supposed to be the just reward) which is compared to an actual reward. When the actual reward falls short of the expected reward, the individual is likely to express feelings of injustice. Feelings of justice occur when the expected reward is equal to the actual reward. However, the theory did not specify what would happen if the actual reward was greater than the expected reward. Would the recipient experience guilt, as equity theory contends (Adams, 1965)? Jasso's theory does not offer an answer to this question.

Individual differences play an important role in this model. Jasso (1994) contends that although two individuals may have identical notions of the just wage, they may differ in the propensity to introduce the just wage as a topic of conversation. Similarly, "two individuals may reach identical justice evaluations about a particular situation, but one may express the judgment with greater emphasis and intensity than the other" (369). Such individual differences in justice judgments may influence subsequent attitudes and behaviors. In addition to individual variables, social and cultural factors play an important role in this model. "There is reason to believe that the process by which individuals form their notions of justice is attentive to features of the social environment that may differ across societies and that may change over time" (403). In this model of distributive justice, justice evaluations vary as the logarithm of the actual share of a good to the perceived just reward:

$$\text{Justice evaluation} = \ln \frac{\text{actual share}}{\text{just share}}$$

Jasso (1980) makes a distinction between *quality goods* and *quantity goods,* where quality goods are nonadditive and nontransferable (charm, health) and quantity goods are additive and transferable. She contends that all members of a social aggregate value the same good, and that the just reward may be considered as the arithmetic mean of the distribution of a good within a social aggregate.

Randall and Mueller (1995) applied this theory in a field setting on a sample of nurses. They found that the more individuals perceive justice in their own involvement in decision making (procedural justice evaluations) and in the distribution of workplace rewards (distributive justice evaluations), the more satisfied they are with their jobs, committed they are to the place of employment, and likely they are to intend to remain employed with that organization. According to Greenberg and Cohen (1982), Jasso's theory focuses on an individual's evaluation of the fairness of his or her own share of a good, not an evaluation of others' shares. Greenberg (1987a) notes that Jasso's theory ignores the outside comparisons in justice evaluations altogether, and defined justice in terms of the comparisons people make between their actual share of goods and their beliefs about a just share. Finally, this theory does not give much attention to reactions following feelings of injustice, contrary to relative deprivation theory (Crosby, 1976, 1982, 1984).

RELATIVE DEPRIVATION THEORY

Relative deprivation is a state experienced by the victim of inequity (Crosby and Gonzalez-Intal, 1984). "Deprivation is an attitude, a feeling of discontent, or perceived injustice" (Martin, 1984, 97). Martin identified three essential elements to the theory of relative deprivation:

1. the objective distribution of outcomes;

2. the choice of a comparative referent (like in equity theory); and

3. a feeling of deprivation.

People feel resentment only when they think they deserve better outcomes (Crosby, 1976). Fine (1979) shares this view by suggesting that people often experience a sense of injustice only when a new ideology makes existing circumstances seem unjustified. "Resentment is a feeling of indignant displeasure or persistent ill will at something regarded as a wrong, insult, or injury and implies anger directed toward a social target" (Folger, 1993, 162).

The concept of relative deprivation can be traced back to the early work of Stouffer et al. (1949) [quoted in Crosby, 1984; Crosby and Gonzalez-Intal, 1984; Greenberg, 1990a], who found that black soldiers stationed in the South felt more satisfied with military life than those stationed in the North, even though economic conditions in the North were better than in the South. They also found that airmen were more dissatisfied with the promotion system than were military policemen, although they had a more rapid promotion system than their police counterparts. Early works on relative deprivation began with Merton and Rossi (1957), Davis (1959), Runciman (1966), and Gurr (1970). In Merton and Rossi's conception, people's expectations about what they would like to possess and should possess derive from explicit or implicit comparisons to other people. This view is similar to that of Davis, whose model distinguishes between *haves* and *have-nots*. When a *have-not* compares his or her situation with that of a *have*, he or she experiences relative deprivation. However, when the person is the *have*, he or she experiences relative gratification. Runciman introduced a distinction between *egoistical deprivation* and *fraternal deprivation*. Egoistical deprivation occurs when the individual feels deprived in comparison with other members in his or her group, while fraternal deprivation occurs when the individual feels his or her group is deprived in comparison with other groups. A doubly deprived individual experiences both egoistical and fraternal deprivation.

According to Gurr (1968, 1104), relative deprivation refers to "actors' perceptions of discrepancy between their value expectations (the goods and conditions of the life to which they believe they are justifiably entitled) and their value capabilities (the amount of those goods and conditions that they think they are able to get and keep)." His model identified three types of deprivation:

1. *Aspirational deprivation*. Occurs when expectations about deserved outcomes accelerate more rapidly than do individuals' capabilities of meeting these expectations.

2. *Decremental deprivation*. Occurs when an individual's expectations remain constant over time while his or her actual capabilities decline.

3. *Progressive deprivation*. The individual's capabilities decline, while his or her expectations accelerate.

Gurr's model of relative deprivation was limited to political systems. Crosby (1976, 1982, 1984) develops a more systematic model, in which perceptions play an important role. "People's feelings of deprivation, discontent, grievance, or resentment often do not relate in a simple, direct, or isomorphic way to their objective situations" (1984, 52). Crosby (1984) identifies two trends in the current research on relative deprivation:

1. People feel aggrieved when their present condition is not as good as they want and not as good as they think it ought to be.

2. Disadvantaged people appear much more prone to recognize that their group suffers more than to recognize that they personally suffer.

In her study of women in the workforce, Crosby (1982) suggested a new approach of relative deprivation, in which the extent of resentment is predicted by two variables: wanting and future expectations. The greater the discrepancy between what one has and what one wants, the greater the discontent. Similarly, the greater the discrepancy between what one has and what one feels one deserves, the greater the resentment. This new approach contends that people experience deprivation when they perceive a discrepancy between actual outcomes and desired outcomes, or the outcomes they deserve.

Resentment is the basic emotional concomitant of relative deprivation. Its behavioral consequences, which may be directed toward either the self or toward society, and may be either constructive or destructive, are stressed symptoms, self-improvement, violence against society, or constructive change of society (Crosby, 1984). Reactions due to relative deprivation can be directed internally at oneself or externally at the system (Cowherd and Levine, 1992). Five conditions are necessary for relative deprivation to occur (Crosby, 1984). One must:

1. want the object;

2. see that another possesses the object;

3. feel that he or she deserves the object;

4. think it is feasible to obtain the object; and

5. lack a sense of responsibility for failure to possess the object.

Rhodebeck (1981, 245) developed the concept of group deprivation, which refers to the "negative feeling that group members have about the situation of their group as a whole, regardless of their own situation within the group." Crosby (1982) extends this concept to groups to whom the individual does not belong. Smith, Spears, and Oyen (1994, 296) suggest that "personal advantage can reduce one's own feelings of deprivation compared to collective deprivation, and leads subjects to interpret general feelings of deprivation in terms of personal advantage rather than collective disadvantage when group membership is primed." This result confirms previous findings by Wright, Taylor, and Moghaddam (1990), who found that personal advantage reduced feelings of collective deprivation.

This discussion of theories of distributive justice has illustrated that people do care about the fairness of the outcomes they receive in an exchange relationship. When they believe that these outcomes are fair, they are likely to feel fairly treated. However, any discrepancy between the outcomes received and the inputs is likely to lead to feelings of inequity and deprivation. To the extent that people do care about the fairness of their outcomes, distributive justice will remain an important area of inquiry in organizational justice. For instance, Crosby and Gonzalez-Intal (1984) note that relative deprivation and equity theory are the two major social psychological approaches of the study of felt distributive injustice. However, as stated by Cropanzano and Randall (1993, 9), "outcomes are not the only relevant issue to an individual; the way one is treated is equally important." Although distributive justice theories have enhanced our understanding of organizational justice, they have neglected the context in which rewards are allocated. A better understanding of justice issues in organizations must go beyond the fairness of outcome distributions and include the formal procedures underlying these distributions.

2

Procedural Justice

Procedural justice refers to the fairness of the rules and procedures by which rewards are distributed (Alexander and Ruderman, 1987). Procedural justice involves the formal characteristics of a system (Folger, Konovsky, and Cropanzano, 1992). "A distribution is a result, whereas procedures are part of the causal network which generates that result" (Leventhal, Karuza, and Fry, 1980, 169). Rawls (1971) considers procedural justice as an end in itself. He contends that procedural fairness also presumes a demonstrated respect for human dignity, for treatment of people in a humane fashion. "The experience of procedural justice (or procedural injustice) is a profound feature of social life, and one that is worthy of study in its own right" (Lind and Tyler, 1988, 93). Underlying the importance of procedural justice, Greenberg (1987a) argues that it is the most promising organizational justice research area. He (1990b) identified three components of procedural justice:

1. formal characteristics of procedures;
2. explanation of procedures and decision making, and
3. interpersonal treatment.

Folger and Konovsky (1989, 126) suggest that procedures can be interpreted at two levels—instrumental (as means) and ends (as symbolic outcomes):

Instrumentally, procedures are means to the ends of distributive justice as when procedures used for allocation decisions about raises include ways of accurately measuring performance . . . As ends, procedures provide intangible outcomes such as respect . . . Such procedural actions treat human beings as ends rather than means and treat them as entitled to respect and concern that are symbolic outcomes of how a decision making process is implemented, regardless of what tangible outcomes are provided.

According to Cropanzano, Kacmar, and Bozerman (1995), a fair organization is one characterized by procedures that ensure such things as voice, due process, advance notice, and so forth. The literature on procedural justice is dominated by four theories: the self-interest model (Thibaut and Walker, 1975, 1978), the procedural preferences model (Leventhal, Karuza, and Fry, 1980), the value-expressive model (Tyler, 1987), and the group-value model (Lind and Tyler, 1988).

THE SELF-INTEREST MODEL

Thibaut and Walker (1975) developed a model of procedural justice emphasizing the roles of process control and decision control. "The self-interest model suggests that people seek control over decisions because they are fundamentally concerned with their outcomes" (Lind and Tyler, 1988, 222). This implies that people prefer to have control about decisions and processes affecting their lives. Experimental studies, mostly in the legal sector, validated these assumptions (Thibaut and Walker, 1975). "Process control refers to control over the development and selection of information that will constitute the basis for resolving the dispute," and decision control refers to the "degree to which any one of the participants may unilaterally determine the outcome of the dispute" (Thibaut and Walker, 1978, 546). Control over the process, however, refers to control over the development and selection of information that will constitute the basis for resolving the dispute.

According to Thibaut and Walker (1975), a procedural system designed to achieve distributive justice will function best if process control is assigned to the disputants. Their procedural justice model identifies five major elements in the procedural process:

1. *Autocratic.* A procedure in which decision control and process control are vested into the decision maker.

2. *Arbitration.* Also known as an adversarial system, arbitration is a procedure allowing the participants to have control over the process, but the decision control is vested in the third party.

3. *Mediation.* A procedure in which the third party can influence the process, but not the decision.

4. *Moot.* A procedure in which the third party can influence neither the process nor the decision.

5. *Bargaining.* In this procedure, there is no third party involved in either the decision control or the process control. The two parties negotiate their deal in setting their own norms.

People seek voice in the decision process because it allows them to influence the outcomes. Underlying the importance of process control, Thibaut and Walker (1975) note that who makes the decision in situations of high conflict is less important to evaluations of fairness than who controls the process through which that decision is made. According to Lind and Tyler (1988), although Thibaut and Walker's theory focuses on legal issues, its basic assumptions could be applied in organizational settings. The authors also argue that Thibaut and Walker's model is based on a self-interest model of the person and did not include issues of trust (see Tyler and Degoey, 1995).

Lind and Tyler (1988) recognize the importance of Thibaut and Walker's model. They contend that "one of the great contributions of Thibaut and Walker is that they saw clearly and so early that knowledge of the psychology of procedural justice might have critical importance in a world where resource constraints dictate that routes to satisfy depend on something other than favorable outcomes" (26). The self-interest model suggests that people try to maximize their personal gain when interacting with others. "According to the informed self-interest model, whether we are speaking of a social group, a political system, or a work organization, people join and remain in that group because they believe that they gain in the long run" (223).

Despite the importance of decision control, Tyler (1987) argues that people value process control even when it is not linked to decision control. According to Lind and Tyler (1988), the self-interest model is an egoistic conception of the person. Tyler, Degoey, and Smith (1996) argue that an instrumental model of procedural justice is incomplete in that procedural justice judgments influence a wide variety of group-oriented attitudes and behaviors, as well as self-esteem. Tyler (1987) developed a value-expressive model, emphasizing the importance of voice in the decision process.

THE VALUE-EXPRESSIVE MODEL

Recognizing the role of process control in justice evaluations, Tyler (1987, 1994) and Tyler, Rasinski, and Spodick (1985) developed a value-expressive model of procedural justice. This model suggests that "disputants want to have voice because they value having the chance to state their case irrespective of whether their statement influences the decisions of authorities" (Tyler, 1987, 333). Voice refers to the extent to which an employee expresses his or her views to decision makers prior to the final decision (Daly and Geyer, 1994; Folger, 1977; Lind and Tyler, 1988). High voice procedures are seen as just because they tend to secure favorable or equitable outcomes (Early and Lind, 1987). People value the opportunity to voice their opinion because it provides them the chance to influence others' decisions (Brett, 1986; Leventhal, 1980; Thibaut and Walker, 1975).

Lind and Tyler (1988) also notice that procedures allowing voice are perceived as fair because they provide opportunities for participation in group processes; and because the opportunity to exercise voice is a visible sign of group membership. They identified four variables in the self-interest model:

1. the favorability of the procedure to the perceiver;
2. the amount of control over outcomes afforded by the perceiver;
3. the fairness of the outcomes provided by the procedure; and
4. the consistency with which the procedure is applied across people.

People view more favorably procedures that either directly advance their own interest or allow them to use the procedure to secure positive outcomes (Lind and Tyler, 1988). In addition, having voice increases perceptions of fairness. Lissak (1983) found that people exposed to the voice procedure gave higher procedural ratings than did those exposed to the no-voice procedure. Tyler, Rasinski, and Spodik (1985, 79) argue that the "chance to speak has value in itself. That value appears unrelated to the influence of voice on the decisions made."

Katz (1960) first suggested the value expressive function, which states that under some circumstances people may find the opportunity to express themselves rewarding in and of itself. However, if people's input is solicited but ignored, voice is void of meaning; individuals will not feel a sense of indirect control or of status and respect (Korsgard, Schweiger, and Sapienza, 1995). "People perceive a voice procedure as fairer than a mute procedure in situations involving job recruitment or budget decision making, even when a decision is unfavorable to them" (Bies and Shapiro, 1988, 682). One of the most potent determinants of the procedural fairness of a social decision making procedure is the extent to which those affected by the decision are allowed to participate to its enactment.

The value-expressive model presents an instrumental view of justice evaluations. By having control over the process, people intend to influence decisions (see Shapiro, 1993). McFarlin and Sweeney (1996) found support for the value-expressive model, that having a say does matter, independent of whether or not one has actual control over decisions. As they put it, one clear indicant of procedural justice for an organization is to have some mechanisms in place which will see to it that workers do have a say about things that happen at work.

People are not only interested in having control over the decision process, but they are also concerned with the interpersonal treatment they receive and their status within the group or the organization. Rather than engaging only in a relatively simple process of determining if and how procedures benefit the self, individuals also take into account the symbolic meaning of their treatment as a group member (Stroesser and Heuer, 1996). Tyler (1994, 85) also argued that the "desire for control is not only a potential motive for wanting procedural justice, but it may also motivate concerns for justice in interactions with others." This latter issue is addressed by the group-value model of procedural justice (Lind and Tyler, 1988).

THE GROUP-VALUE MODEL

Tyler (1994) refers to two psychological theories to explain why people seek justice: the first, social-exchange resource model, argues that people want to maximize the resources they obtain from social interactions, a goal they believe is facilitated by following rules of distributive and procedural justice; and the second, identity-based relational model, suggests that people attempt to maintain high status within groups and use the justice of their experiences to evaluate their group status. The group-value model (GVM) contends that people value membership within a group and prefer to be respected and considered as full members (Lind and Tyler, 1988; Tyler, 1994). The model suggests that people value the information they receive which helps them to define themselves and view themselves favorably (Brockner, Tyler, and Cooper-Schneider, 1992). Two elements are important in this model: group identity (elements that distinguish the group from other social entities), and group procedures that govern much thought and behavior with respect to groups, organizations, or society (Lind and Tyler, 1988). Lind and Tyler, who developed this model, consider that the neutrality of the decision making, trust in the third party, and the information the experience communicates about social standing, influence both procedural preferences and judgments of procedural justice.

"The perceived fairness in which procedures are carried out may provide information about the trustworthiness of authorities" (Tyler and Degoey, 1995, 63). Lind and Tyler (1988) suggest that justice judgments' effects on factors such as choice and voice depend on three considerations:

1. the extent to which the factor is in accord with the values of the society or group using the procedure;
2. the extent to which the factor carries symbolic implications for the individual's status in the group or society; and
3. the extent to which the object of the voice or choice is seen as important or central to fundamental process issues in the group.

Tyler (1989, 837) suggests that people are concerned about their long-term social relationships with the authorities or institutions acting as third parties, and do not view their relationships with third parties as a one "shot deal." "Because people in organizations focus on their long-term association with authorities, they expect organizations to use neutral decision-making procedures enacted by trustworthy authorities and to treat them with respect, dignity, and politeness so that, over time, all group members will benefit fairly from being members of the group."

People also learn to compromise with others when they join a group. "When people join and remain in groups, they come to recognize that other people's outcomes or priorities must sometimes be accepted and their own desires must sometimes be delayed or foregone. This is the case because others will remain in the group only if their own concerns are sometimes addressed" (Lind and Tyler, 1988, 223). The group-value model contends that many procedural values and beliefs are instilled through socialization. New members of groups learn procedural values and beliefs from older members (Lind and Tyler, 1988). People define themselves through their membership in various collectives (Tajfel and Turner, 1979). "Unfair procedures symbolize to group members that the collective has little respect for their dignity"

(Brockner and Wiesenfeld, 1996, 200). When procedures are unfair, people may consider their relationships with the collective (organization, group, etc.) as transactional. Two elements—group identity and group procedures—govern much thought and behavior with respect to groups, organizations, or society. Group identity refers to the distinction from other groups or social entities, and group procedures refer to how people are treated within groups (Lind and Tyler, 1988).

Giacobble-Miller (1995) conducted a field study on a sample of ninety school superintendents and seventy-four union presidents, testing the predictive power of the group-value and self-interest models. Results showed that the group-value variables of perceived neutrality of, and trust in, third parties predicted procedural justice judgments. Process control also predicted procedural justice judgments, whereas decision control did not. Neither of the two models predicted distributive justice judgments.

Treatment by the leader sends an important message to group members about their status within a group. Tyler (1989) suggests that if a leader treats a work group member with respect or disrespect, information about the member's status is communicated both to that member and other group members who identify with the individual. One of the practical implications of the group-value model is that employees are more likely to view management's authority and its decisions as legitimate, to the extent that fair procedures are used to make fair decisions (Tyler and Lind, 1992). Tyler, Degoey, and Smith (1996) suggest that fair procedures and treatment communicate information about: (1) the degree to which individuals are respected members of their groups, and (2) the degree to which they can feel pride in their group membership. Unfair treatment indicates marginality and disrespect (Tyler, 1994; Tyler and Lind, 1992), whereas fair treatment indicates a positive, respected position within the group (Tyler, 1989; Tyler, Degoey, and Smith, 1996). Tyler (1989) and Lind (1995) note that judgments of procedural fairness are dominated by three types of relational judgments about authorities: neutrality, trustworthiness, and status recognition:

1. neutrality involves assessments of the degree to which decision-making procedures are unbiased, honest, and promote decisions based on evidence;

2. trustworthiness involves assessments of the motives of authorities' judgments about their benevolence and concern for the needs of those with whom they deal; and

3. status recognition involves assessments of politeness, treatment with dignity, and respect for rights and entitlements due to every group member.

According to Lind (1995, 88), "people use justice judgments as both mediators and moderators of the decision to accept organizational decisions and procedures. Justice judgments mediate between impressions of process and expected outcomes on one hand and the acceptance of authorities' decisions, policies, and procedures on the other." The author additionally contends that justice judgments also depend on the three components: status recognition, benevolence, and neutrality: "Judgments of the fairness of procedures will rest far more on impressions of status recognition, benevolence, and neutrality gleaned from interactions with authorities than on evaluations of the outcomes or likely outcomes of those interactions" (91). The importance of procedures is also recognized by Leventhal, Karuza, and Fry (1980), who developed a procedural preferences model.

THE PROCEDURAL PREFERENCES MODEL

This model is an extension of Leventhal's justice judgment model. As people choose allocations which lead to the goal previously set, they tend to select the procedures which help them achieve their goals. Leventhal, Karuza, and Fry (1980) identified six procedural justice rules:

1. *Consistency.* This dimension implies that procedures must be consistent to ensure fairness. Inconsistent procedures may raise feelings of injustice.

2. *Bias suppression.* Procedures must be developed and implemented without considering the self-interests of those who elaborated them.

3. *Rule of accuracy.* Procedures must be based on accurate information.

4. *Rule of correctability.* Procedures must allow room for correcting decisions once they are made and perceived as wrong. This rule is similar to the appeal procedures of the legal system.

5. *Rule of representativeness.* Procedures must integrate the interests of all parties involved in the process. This rule implies participation as it is known in the management literature.

6. *Rule of ethicality.* Procedures must follow moral and ethical standards.

According to Leventhal, Karuza, and Fry (1980), procedural rules, like distributive rules, are weighted according to the objective pursued by the decision maker. Procedures contain seven structural components:

1. select agents to gather information and make the decision;

2. set ground rules and establish criteria for receiving an allocation;

3. gather information;

4. define the decision;

5. process appeals from the decision;

6. safeguard the procedure by monitoring and sanctioning the behavior of those who participate in the procedure; and

7. provide mechanisms for changing the procedure when it is not working properly.

Following these rules is likely to increase the perceived fairness of participants. When these procedural rules are clearly specified and the participants have a say in the decision process, they are likely to accept not only the process, but also the decisions derived from it. Folger and Bies (1989) identified seven procedural elements important to managers:

1. giving adequate consideration to employees' viewpoints;

2. suppressing biases;

3. applying decision-making criteria consistently across employees;

4. providing timely feedback to employees after the decision;

5. providing justification for the decision;

6. being truthful in communication; and

7. treating employees with courtesy and civility.

These seven rules are similar to Leventhal's (1976, 1980) procedural justice rules. For instance, Folger and Bies (1989) note that when decision makers are honest in communications, people are more likely to infer that the underlying procedure is fair than when the decision makers are dishonest. Alexander and Ruderman (1987) identified three measures of procedural justice: metaprocedures, allocation procedures, and appeal procedures. Metaprocedural activities precede the allocation stage and consist of those values, rules, and processes that influence the establishment of allocation procedures and/or appeal procedures. Allocation procedures refer to those rules and procedures actually used in distributing a particular outcome or reward. Finally, appeal procedures refer to those processes (authorized or informal) by which recipients can attempt to change the allocation that has occurred. Applied in organizational settings, procedural justice is enhanced by the existence of formal appeal, feedback, explanation, and grievance procedures. For instance, Konovsky and Cropanzano (1993) suggest the use of advance notice in administering a drug test. When such administration is one of the criteria of the recruitment process, potential applicants should be informed in advance; doing so increases the perceived fairness of the recruitment process. The authors found that participants considered drug testing fair in presence of advance notice.

In addition to distributive and procedural theories of justice, some models, especially referent cognitions theory, have attempted to integrate these two aspects of justice. Referent cognitions theory implies a direct relationship between procedures and outcomes. "To the extent that procedures qualify the meaning of outcomes (and reactions to them), it would be essential for conceptualizations of justice in organizations to incorporate procedural variables" (Greenberg, 1987b, 60). Sashkin and Williams (1990) also suggest the combination of distributive justice and procedural justice. They contend that only when employees believe that managers value people are they likely to consider management actions fair. Perceptions of procedural justice can affect perceptions and reactions to distributive justice (Folger, Rosenfield, and Robinson, 1983). Similarly, Folger (1987) notes that distributive justice and procedural justice are interrelated, such that perceptions of one can influence perceptions of the other.

Joy and Witt (1992, 299) also underscored the interdependence of distributive justice and procedural justice: "Across most situations, when individuals perceive fairness in how decisions are made, they are more likely to perceive the outcomes as fair than when the procedures are unfair. Similarly, when individuals perceive a fair outcome, they are more likely to assume that fair procedures led to that outcome." Tyler (1994) found a positive relationship between distributive justice and procedural justice. However, Folger (1987, 150) notes that "although perceptions of procedural justice can influence perceptions of distributive justice, application of the fairest possible procedures does not define distributive justice." Therefore, the effect of procedures on perceptions of outcome fairness is relative, not absolute. According to Folger, distributive justice and procedural justice can be evaluated on independent grounds, such that the two types of fairness need not coincide.

REFERENT COGNITIONS THEORY (RCT)

Referent cognitions involve a simulation model that starts with a mental "undoing" of the present or past by focusing not on existing circumstances, but on imaginable alternatives, then the simulation is run (Folger, Rosenfield, and Robinson, 1983). When people contemplate the treatment they have received from others, they evaluate it in relation to standards of comparison (referent outcomes) drawn from any of several potential sources, including their own past outcomes, the outcomes of others, and ideal conceptions about entitlements and rewards (Folger and Baron, 1996). Referent cognitions theory contends that justification of procedures plays an important role in reactions toward outcomes. A change in procedures is directly related to a change in outcomes.

Referent cognitions theory builds on the early work on simulation heuristic (Kahneman and Tversky, 1982). In light of the heuristic model, individuals act and react according to mental processes they have previously elaborated. Folger, Rosenfield, and Robinson (1983, 273) found that "when procedures are changed, people will be dissatisfied if their outcomes fall short of what might reasonably be expected under some alternative procedure, but only when there is insufficient justification for use of the current procedure." Referent cognitions theory combines equity theory's emphasis on outcome with the emphasis on process (Folger, 1993). Folger considers it a two-factor theory, with an outcome factor and a process factor. He argues that for resentment to occur, one must have a combination of outcome and process. Resentment of an agent can stem from dissatisfaction with an outcome, but only in conjunction with the implementation of unfair procedures or other inappropriate conduct by the agent. The necessity of conjunctive conditions implies an outcome/process interaction as a fundamental referent cognitions theory prediction. According to Folger, Rosenfield, and Robinson, the presence of three elements is necessary for referent cognitions to occur:

1. outcomes must be below the desired level;
2. there must be instigations to thoughts about outcomes that would be at the desired level; and
3. there must be an absence of sufficient reasons why actual outcomes are not as high as referent outcomes.

"Referent cognitions theory predicts resentment as a form of hostile feeling toward someone responsible for one's own unfavorable outcomes, someone whose wrongdoing was instrumental in bringing about such outcomes" (Folger and Martin, 1986, 532). In an experimental study, Folger and Martin found that individuals whose experimenter followed an acceptable procedure (high-justification conditions) showed a level of discontent that was equally minimal, regardless of whether actual outcomes were concordant or discordant with previous expectations. However, more anger and resentment were expressed by high-referent, low-justification subjects than by low-referent, low-justification subjects under an arbitrary experimenter. In another experimental study, Cropanzano and Folger (1989) found that when the procedure involved a decision by the subject, feelings of unfair treatment were noticeably absent, regardless of whether the subjects would have won or lost had their nonincentive scores counted.

Under appropriate conditions, referent cognitions theory contends, unfairness may lead to strong feelings of anger, resentment, and an accompanying desire for revenge (Folger and Baron, 1996). By its emphasis both on outcome distribution and procedures, referent cognitions theory presents an integration of distributive justice and procedural justice. As noted by Cropanzano and Folger (1989), referent cognitions theory offers the basis for a true integration of distributive fairness and procedural fairness. They contend that a person's willingness to press claims of unfair treatment, in particular, stems not only from having a reason to believe that the outcome received is unfavorable, but also from having a reason to associate that unfavorable outcome with someone else's actions rather than his or her own actions. An important factor increasing referent cognitions is participation (or lack of participation). "The absence of participation makes it easier for people to imagine ways their outcomes might have been more favorable. Thus the lesson for administrators is that if people do not participate in decisions, there may be little room to prevent them from assuming that things would have been better if I had been in charge" (Cropanzano and Folger, 1989, 298).

According to Brockner and Wiesenfeld (1996), the joint presence of unfair procedures and unfavorable outcomes elicits greater resentment than any other combination of conditions. They contend that one may predict the favorability of future outcomes based on the fairness (or unfairness) of current procedures. Referring to the rule of consistency (Leventhal, 1976), they argue that "procedures used to make resource allocation decisions usually are perceived to be relatively stable and enduring; consequently, people use information about procedures to make inferences about their longer term outcomes" (193). The authors focused on the integration of distributive and procedural justice. They suggest that "our central thesis is that whereas perceived outcome favorability differs from individuals' perceptions of procedural fairness, their impact cannot be studied in isolation from one another" (190). This assumption refers to Cropanzano and Folger's (1989) suggestion that perceptions of fairness of outcomes and procedures work together to create a sense of justice.

A full understanding of fairness cannot be achieved by examining the two constructs separately. Rather, one needs to consider the interaction between outcomes and procedures (Cropanzano and Folger, 1989). Folger (1993) suggested a revised model of referent cognitions theory, which he named the *dual-obligation model*. This new version of RCT de-emphasizes the causal link between an agent in an authority role and the outcomes received by someone subject to that authority. This new model stresses the crucial elements that all interpersonal exchanges have in common, "things being exchanged and persons doing the exchanging rather than the causal role of the social agent who acts as decision maker" (Folger, 1993, 174). Folger notes that the revised version of RCT identifies things being exchanged as the first factor of a two-factor model. The second factor, the agent's role, requires greater attention in an expanded approach that focuses on the obligations of that role. This model combines both distributive and procedural justice. It also implies a moral obligation on the part of the agent. Folger underscores this aspect by stating that: "I contend that in the context of employment, the agent's moral obligations toward the employee entail more than fair treatment with respect to the wages and benefits given in exchange for labor, and more than fair treatment with respect to the implementation of policies and procedures that determine those levels of compensation" (174). Such a treatment indicates to the employee that he or she is respected. It also signifies that the employee is recognized as a full member of the organization. For Folger, there is a moral obligation to treat an employee with sufficient dignity as a person.

Moral obligations imply that agents cannot act capriciously, nor can they be inconsiderate in their relationships with employees. As Folger (1993, 175) puts it, "accountability characteristically goes with responsibility, thus calling for consideration of the agent's conduct." Treatment with respect and dignity refers to the interpersonal aspect of procedural justice (Greenberg, 1990a). Tyler and Bies (1990) suggest a broader approach to procedural justice. They contend that once a decision maker enacts a procedure, it is an interpersonal process that employees evaluate in terms of procedural justice. Their broader view of procedural justice contains four elements: (1) the decision maker's conduct, (2) the attribution of social construction of procedural justice, (3) the human side of procedural justice, and (4) the conduct, community, and procedural justice. This includes considerations relative to interpersonal treatment. Although the number of empirical investigations on organizational justice is increasing, few have integrated the interactional aspect of justice. Bies and Moag (1986) note that historically, justice researchers have neglected interactional concerns and restricted their attention to an analysis of outcomes and procedures as bases of fairness judgments.

3

Interactional Justice

Interactional justice refers to the social aspects of procedural justice (Greenberg, 1993b). "Interactional justice refers to the quality of interpersonal treatment people receive during the enactment of organizational procedures" (Bies and Moag, 1986, 44). Shapiro (1993) defined interactional justice in a broader sense, considering it a social exchange between two parties. Although some authors (Greenberg, 1993b) have considered interactional justice as social aspects of procedural justice, I treat the two dimensions of procedural justice and interactional justice as distinct, although correlated (Beugré and Baron, 1997). Current organizational literature differentiates interactional justice from procedural justice.

INTERACTIONAL JUSTICE VS. PROCEDURAL JUSTICE

Bies and Moag (1986) and Bies and Shapiro (1987) suggest that interactional justice should be understood as separated from procedural justice since it represents the enactment of procedures rather than the development of procedures themselves. Procedural justice refers to the degree to which formal procedures are present and used in the organization, whereas interactional justice refers to the fairness of the manner in which the procedures are carried out. Tyler and Bies (1990) suggest that the so-called interactional justice may be best understood as an interpersonal aspect of procedural justice. For the authors, the concept of procedural justice should be broadened enough to encompass interpersonally-based procedures. They prefer to use the term "interpersonal context of procedural justice" instead of interactional justice, and suggest that procedural fairness judgments are influenced, in part, by the interpersonal treatment one receives. However, Mikula (1980) views interpersonal treatment as an independent aspect of justice evaluations which must be different from the concept of procedures. Similarly, Cropanzano and Randall (1993) contend that individuals expect to be treated in a polite and respectful fashion and do not respond favorably to insults and discourteous behavior. Greenberg (1993b) identifies two classes of justice that focus on socially fair treatment: informational justice and interpersonal justice.

TWO DIMENSIONS OF INTERACTIONAL JUSTICE

Informational Justice

Informational justice refers to the social determinants of procedural justice, the adequacy of the information used to explain how decisions are made, and the thoroughness of the accounts. Informational justice may be sought by providing knowledge about the procedures that demonstrate regard for people's concerns (Greenberg, 1993b). To the extent that people are informed about procedures, they are likely to perceive that they are fairly treated. Bies and Moag (1986) and Greenberg (1993b, 1994) have underscored the importance of information in individuals' perceptions of fair treatment. Working on a sample of M.B.A. job applicants, Bies and Moag (1986) found that job candidates believed that corporate recruiters treated them fairly to the extent that they presented honest and candid information and reasonable justifications for the decisions made. When job applicants received quick feedback on their chances, they judged the recruiting procedures to be fairer than when feedback was delayed.

Greenberg (1994) also found that providing a great deal of information about a smoking ban's necessity (e.g., informational justice), and announcing it in a manner that showed considerable awareness of the inconvenience (interpersonal justice), influenced the degree to which employees embraced such a potentially threatening policy. Brockner, Konovsky, Cooper-Schneider, Folger, Martin, and Bies (1994) found that if layoffs are perceived to be procedurally fair, the reactions of layoff victims, survivors, and "lame ducks" (employees who knew they would soon be laid off) were affected by outcome-related factors. The authors also found that outcome negativity was significantly, inversely related to organizational trust and support when procedural fairness was low, but was not so related when procedural fairness was high. This conclusion confirms previous findings that justification for an adverse decision can lessen negative consequences associated with that decision (Bies and Shapiro, 1988). Greenberg (1993b) found that the degree of stealing by employees whose wages were cut was moderated by the validity of information given and the degree of interpersonal sensitivity shown to them. Efficient communications influence perceptions of justice.

Folger and Bies (1989) contend that when decision makers are honest in their communications, people are more likely to infer that the underlying procedure is fair than when the decision makers are dishonest. However, some researchers suggested that the capacity of explanation and information to mitigate negative reactions was overestimated. According to Shapiro (1991), the boundary conditions of explanations mitigating effect include the perceived honesty of the explainer, the severity of the news, and the type of negative emotion experienced by the person receiving the explanation. Nevertheless, giving explanations and information is an important aspect of interpersonal justice.

Interpersonal Justice

Interpersonal justice refers to the social interactions between an individual and others in an organizational setting or a social exchange. It refers to the considerateness and courtesy shown by the partners responsible for dividing available rewards (Folger and Baron, 1996). In an organizational setting, others may include an employee's colleagues, as well as superiors and subordinates. Perceived fairness of the relationship between him or her and these others is the focus of interpersonal justice. Tajfel and Turner (1979) contend that people value relationships because it is through them that they develop their self-identity and self-worth. Relationships give people the opportunity to validate the correctness of their beliefs and behaviors and to feel accepted, respected, and valued. Fair treatment by the other party symbolizes that an individual is being dealt with in a dignified and respectful way, thereby bolstering his or her sense of self-identity and self-worth (Brockner, Tyler, and Cooper-Schneider, 1992).

Although informational and interpersonal justice are two components of interactional justice, they are different, in that "informational justice focuses on knowledge of the procedures leading to outcomes, whereas interpersonal justice focuses on the consequences of those outcomes directly" (Greenberg, 1993a, 84). In studying citizens' interactions with political authorities, Tyler and Folger (1980) and Tyler (1988) found that citizens placed great value on being treated politely and having respect shown for their rights. The effects of interpersonal justice may be well observed in organizations, units, work groups, and so forth. Frequent interactions with a variety of people is an important aspect of organizational life. The quality of interactions with colleagues, superiors, or subordinates, may influence an individual's perceptions of fairness, although this topic has been neglected by organizational justice scholars. In an era where teamwork is valued and encouraged, understanding interactional fairness may contribute to improving social exchanges in organizations.

SOCIAL ACCOUNTS AND INTERACTIONAL JUSTICE

Research on organizational justice (Bies and Moag, 1986; Bies and Shapiro, 1987, 1988) stipulates that explanations tend to increase perceptions of fairness. The literature on organizational justice identified several types of explanations, ranging from causal accounts (Bies, 1987) to justifications (Daly, 1995).

The Impact of Explanations on Perceptions of Fairness

Social Accounts

A social account is a verbal strategy employed by a person to minimize the apparent severity of the predicament or to convince the audience that the wrongful act is not a fair representation of what the actor is really like as a person (Bies, 1987). Social accounts refer to the explanations, justifications, and apologies made to "ease" the effects of an injustice. They have an importance on the victim's reactions to injustice. Accounts are explanations designed to remove an actor from a predicament (Greenberg, 1990c). Bies (1987) identified four types of social accounts: causal, ideological, referential, and penitential.

Causal Accounts

According to Bies (1987) and Scott and Lyman (1968), a causal account is an explanation containing a reason to mitigate the harmdoer's responsibility. The purpose of a claim of mitigating circumstances is to suggest that any other person would have acted in a similar manner in that situation (Bies, 1987). Causal accounts may influence perceptions of fair treatment. For instance, if the harmdoer provides a causal account and this provision tends to reduce his or her own responsibility, then the victim of a perceived injustice may be less likely to blame him or her (Bies, 1987; Bies and Shapiro, 1987, 1988). To ease the perceived unfairness of organizational downsizing, managers may invoke the state of the economy. Bies (1987, 299) notes that "providing a causal account claiming mitigating circumstances can reduce the expression of moral outrage; however, failure to provide a good account can exacerbate such feelings."

Ideological Accounts

Ideological accounts explain a decision in terms of superordinate goals and principles which guide decision making, such as higher order values (Cobb, Wooten, and Folger, 1995). Bies (1987) notes that an ideological account can manifest itself in one or two ways. First, the decision maker may invoke reasons related to superordinate goals to justify a decision. For instance, a manager may justify a pay cut by relying on the company's survival. I call this action *reframing*, because, rather than minimizing responsibility, "the harmdoer is attempting to explain the action by placing it in a broader framework that will legitimate the action" (Bies, 1987, 300). The second way of expressing an ideological account, which I call *labeling*, refers to an attempt to explain the action or the outcome in more value-laden terms: "By invoking positive value-laden terms to characterize the action or outcome, the harmdoer is hoping that the victim will use a more favorable schema to process the information" (301). Tversky and Kahneman (1981, 458) note that framing of an action sometimes affects the actual experience of its outcomes. They suggest that "framing outcomes in terms of overall wealth or welfare rather than in terms of specific gains and losses may attenuate one's emotional response to an occasional loss." Similarly, they contend that the experience of a change for the worse may vary if the change is framed as an uncompensated loss or as a cost incurred to achieve some benefit.

Referential Accounts

According to Bies (1987), there are three types of referential accounts: social, temporal, and aspirational. He suggests that in referential accounts, the harmdoer may use social comparison to justify the outcome (social referential account), argue that things will be better in the future (temporal referential account), or persuade the "victim" that his or her expectations were unrealistic (aspirational account). Referential accounts are aimed at changing the frame of reference for those affected by a particular decision (Cobb, Wooten, and Folger, 1995). Kahneman and Tversky (1982, 201) suggest the concept of simulation heuristic, whose output is construed as an assessment of the ease with which the model could produce different outcomes, given its initial conditions and operating parameters: "Mental simulation yields a measure of the propensity of one's model of the situation to generate various outcomes, much as the propensities of a statistical model can be assessed by Monte Carlo Technique."

Penitential Accounts

Penitential accounts refer to apologies or statements of regret given by those who might be held directly or indirectly responsible for some harm done to others. Bies (1987, 303) contends that "a penitential account includes a public expression of guilt and a rejection of the bad part of the person responsible for the wrongdoing. A penitential account represents a public enactment of self-retribution." Penitential accounts are also known as apologies (Schlenker, 1980). Apologies are confessions of responsibility for negative events which include some expressions of remorse (Bies, 1987). Why does a decision maker choose a penitential account? The purpose of a penitential account is to ease the potential injustice perceived by the victim. By apologizing, the harmdoer seeks some understanding from the victim. Apologies are an effective means of reducing expressions of anger (Baron, 1990). They also help to convince others that the harmdoer's actions should not be considered a fair representation of what the actor is really like as a person (Schlenker, 1980). According to Greenberg (1990c), apologies may refer to excuses which are designed to deny or minimize responsibility for a predicament. "Excuses are explanations in which individuals acknowledge that their conduct was somehow bad, wrong, or inappropriate, but attempted to minimize their personal responsibility or culpability" (Tetlock, 1985, 215). Greenberg (1991) found that low-rated employees who received apologies for low performance ratings accepted those evaluations as more fair than those who did not receive such apologies.

By suggesting the concept of predicament of moral outrage, which focuses on the behavior of the harmdoer, Bies (1987) addresses the social implications of injustice. For the author, an injustice is not merely a judgment, it represents a violation of justice and fairness norms. Being responsible of such a violation creates predicament for the harmdoer. In violating such norms, the harmdoer is vulnerable to a variety of reactions that are influenced by other people's moral outrage. According to Bies (1987, 299), moral outrage provides a focus for social account: "providing a causal account claiming mitigating circumstances can reduce the expression of moral outrage; the failure to provide a good account can exacerbate such feelings."

Bies (1987) suggests another concept, *liability of injustice*, which refers to the potential reputational consequences that follow from the violation of justice norms. According to Bies, the strategy of social accounts is used by harmdoers to defend themselves against an injustice for which they are responsible. Bies and Shapiro (1987) conducted two laboratory experiments and a field study to analyze the influence of causal accounts on employee behavior. They found that fairness concerns raised about the propriety of a decision maker's behavior during the enactment of procedures were representative for a desire of interactional justice. In another experimental study, Shapiro (1991) found that explanations did mitigate participants' reactions to deceit. The author also found that it was not the type of explanation which was important, but the extent to which the explanation was perceived as adequate. In discussing interactional justice issues in organizational change, Novelli, Kirkman, and Shapiro (1995, 27) suggest that the focus should be on how those who are in positions of authority treat those who are affected by the decision, regardless of the actual outcomes or processes used to determine the outcomes. "From an interactional justice perspective, managers need to guard against treating people in a way that is interpreted as condescending through verbal or nonverbal behaviors."

Justification as a Particular Type of Social Account

Another type of explanation which enhances perceptions of justice is justification (Bies and Shapiro, 1988; Daly, 1995). Justifications are explanations in which the actor takes responsibility for the action, but denies that it has the negative quality that others might attribute to it (Tedeschi and Reiss, 1981). Bies and Shapiro (1988) contend that the provision of an explanation can be helpful, not only in addressing substantive concerns but also in sending a signal that the outcomes and procedures used are, in fact, justifiable. Justifications can enhance perceptions of fairness.

Daly (1995) suggests that the process of explaining decisions in a change context helps employees to adapt to the change, because the lack of explanation is often regarded by employees as unfair, generating resentment toward management and toward the decision. He found that justifications were related to outcome and procedural fairness. However, this relationship was moderated by outcome favorability. The author also found that respondents in the unfavorable outcomes group evidently tended to look for explanations from management in making outcome fairness judgments, whereas respondents in the favorable outcomes group generally did not. It appeared that when outcomes were favorable, justifications were not necessary. This conclusion supported previous findings. Shaver (1985) contends that outcome recipients will assign blame for an action only when the outcomes are negative. In organizations, one may suggest that explanations are needed whenever a decision outcome is likely to be perceived as negative by employees. "The provision of explanations fulfills expectations that those affected by negative decisions deserve an explanation" (Sitkin, Sucliffe, and Reed, 1993, 89).

The term justification is broader than causal account, ideological account, referential account, and penitential account. As stated by Daly (1995) and Greenberg (1990c), a justification is mainly an explanation given for a specific decision. This justification may be conceived as any type of social account. For instance, in implementing a change program, a manager may explain to employees the reasons for the changes. By so doing, the manager may consider the survival of the organization (superordinate goal); argue that the change is needed to remain competitive and survive in the new business setting; or use a referential account statement. The organization changes because everyone in the industry is undertaking changes to become leaner and more competitive. Harmdoers might use justifications as one strategy to restore psychological equity (Walster, Walster, and Berscheid, 1978). According to Greenberg and Folger (1983), information that is openly shared which explains the rationale for an organization decision, showing that it was not made capriciously or maliciously, is likely to enhance perceptions of the fairness of the decision, hence its acceptance.

Characteristics of the Account Provider

Few studies in organizational justice have concerned the impact of the causal account provider on perceptions of fairness. However, there is some evidence that the status or the degree of honesty (or dishonesty) of an account provider may influence how receivers not only perceive the information, but also how they feel treated. For instance, intentional actions which provide negative outcomes may be perceived as unfair, compared to those for which external causes are evoked. Attributions of internal and intentional causality heighten people's sensitivity to injustices (Greenberg, 1990a). Bies and Shapiro (1987, 216) suggest that "if a leader can provide an adequate causal account claiming mitigating circumstances, then he or she may be able to maintain control and authority in the context of apparent impropriety." Bies (1987) and Bies, Shapiro, and Cummings (1988) note that the greater the perceived sincerity of a supervisor's reasons for rejecting workers' requests, the more liked the supervisor was, and the more fair the supervisor's actions were perceived to be. Expressed differently, providing explanations may help to enhance a supervisor's power base rather than reduce it.

Feedback and Perceptions of Interactional Justice

Providing feedback is an important factor contributing to perceptions of fair treatment. Folger and Bies (1989) note that timely feedback enhances perceptions of justice, while unduly late feedback is perceived as unfair. Baron (1993, 165) suggests that negative feedback (or criticism) had a negative impact on perceptions of fairness. The author notes that destructive criticism tends to be perceived as unfair: "When criticism is perceived as being fair, the information it contains is subjected to careful scrutiny and elaborate processing. . . . In contrast, when criticism is perceived as being unfair or unjustified, relatively little processing of the information it contains follows." However, one may notice also that negative feedback *per se* does not count much. This assumption is echoed by Baron: "Where negative feedback is concerned, it is not simply the information that one has performed poorly that matters; the style in which this information is conveyed is important too" (159).

Why does feedback influence perceptions of justice? First, one may contend that people prefer to get information about their actual behaviors. Getting such information helps them to adjust their behaviors and understand what others think about them. Failure to provide such feedback may be perceived as rude and inconsiderate. Sapienza and Korsgaard (1996) conducted an experiment with business students and a field survey of venture capitalists regarding their relations with CEOs of new ventures. The authors considered two aspects of justice: timely feedback (information that allows investors to stay up to date on the performance of the venture), and influence (extent to which venture capitalists affected decisions). They found that timely feedback led to positive attitudes toward the entrepreneurs. Giving information on a timely basis was considered as important by venture capitalists. Van den Bos, Vermont, and Wilke (1997) found that concerns of procedural justice may be more important when people are informed about the procedure first than when they are informed about the procedures second, and concerns about distributive justice may be important when people know about the outcome later.

Perceptions of interpersonal treatment may influence perceptions of systemic justice, that is perceptions of the organization as a fair system. The next section discusses systemic justice, another justice dimension coined by Sheppard, Lewicki, and Minton (1992), Beugré (1996), and Beugré and Baron (1997). Perceptions of how managers treat employees may induce judgments about the fairness of the organization as a system.

SYSTEMIC JUSTICE: A FOURTH DIMENSION OF ORGANIZATIONAL JUSTICE

An organization is beforehand a social system, thus concepts of systems theory (Boulding, 1956; Katz and Kahn, 1978; Von Betallanfy, 1962) may help to understand justice issues in organizations. A system is a set of interacting units (Katz and Kahn, 1978). For Asforth (1992), the focus of systems theory is on the set of the whole, the interplay be-

tween the units, and the units' relationships with the larger environment. As such, systems can induce concerns for fairness (or
unfairness). Is an employee fairly treated by the organization in which
he or she works? "Perceptions of unfairness may threaten the legitimacy of a system" (Asforth, 1992, 377). The author suggests that specific goals encourage a narrow perspective, rationalized means
contribute to rigid procedures, universalistic criteria give rise to imper-
sonality, and so forth. The very attempt to organize a given activity
may lead to structures and processes that undermine the activity,
therefore raising concerns for perceived fairness (or unfairness).

The systemic level of justice concerns the broader organizational
context in which procedures are embedded (Sheppard, Lewicki, and
Minton, 1992). Systemic justice represents a global assessment of the
degree to which the organization itself is fair (Bies and Tripp, 1995). It
deals with the organization as a social entity. Individuals want to feel
that they are being treated fairly by others and, in the workplace context, that they are being treated fairly not only by coworkers and supervisors, but by their organization as well (Folger and Baron, 1996).
However, systemic justice may also apply to particular subsystems
within the organization (e.g., units, departments, pay systems, and
hiring systems). A study of systemic justice should therefore recognize
the existence of subsystems within the organization.

According to Sheppard, Lewicki, and Minton (1992), in addition
to outcomes and procedures, systems themselves may be considered
fair or unfair. The authors describe organizations as multi-interest political systems. They identified three organizational arrangements calling for different practices of organizational justice. First, when
organizations are viewed as serving a single interest, managerial actions and organization systems are evaluated in terms of the degree to
which they effectively and efficiently pursue the achievement of that
single interest's goals. Second, when organizations are viewed as arenas
to structure the interplay of only two or three interests, systems should
be designed to achieve the generation and distribution of resources
fairly across these interest groups. Finally, when organizations are considered as arenas for the interplay of many interests, actions and systems should be evaluated in terms of the degree to which they develop

and permit adequate representation of these many separate interests within the firm. Greenberg (1993a) defined systemic justice by referring it to the variety of procedural justice that is accomplished via structural means. Sheppard, Lewicki, and Minton noted that a system that stays unfair long enough will either fail completely or become subject to external procedural and systemic controls.

According to Sheppard, Lewicki, and Minton (1992), systems are considered unfair when they do not apply similar procedural and distributive solutions across similar situations at different times and across different types of people. People often express feelings about the fairness of the system in which they operate. The authors argued that systemic justice leads to procedural justice (determination of procedures), which leads to distributive justice (fairness of the distribution of outcomes). They also suggested that "for fairness to exist, the procedure must pass tests at three levels: the level of the outcome itself, the procedure that generated and implemented the outcome, and the system within which the outcome and procedure were embedded" (14).

Belief that decisionmaking procedures are fair promotes loyalty and good feeling toward the system (Lind and Tyler 1988). Beugré (1996), and Beugré and Baron (1997) recently identified systemic justice as a distinct component of organizational justice. In a factor analysis, the authors isolated systemic justice as different from distributive justice, procedural justice, and interactional justice. The systemic justice dimension was measured by ten items describing the fairness of the organization as a system or the fairness of its subunits. The authors also found that systemic justice was predicted by distributive justice, procedural justice, and interactional justice.

The discussion of the different theories showed that research should consider at least three dimensions of organizational, distributive, procedural, and interactional justice. Perceptions of fairness at these three dimensions may lead to perceptions of the organization as a fair system. People do care about the outcomes they receive in exchange to their inputs in organizations. To the extent that employees are adequately compensated, they will express feelings of distributive fairness. In addition to the fairness of outcomes, employees do care about the existence of fair formal procedures and methods in the organizations. The existence of formal procedures that guarantee voice and protect employee rights may lead to perceptions of procedural fairness. However, the existence of formal procedures does not guarantee their enactment. Employees prefer to be treated with respect and dignity. Such interpersonal respect may enhance perceptions of interactional justice. As I have noticed, perceptions of fairness at these levels of distributive, procedural, and interactional justice are likely to lead to perceptions of the whole organization as a fair system. Perceptions of justice do not only depend on what managers do to employees, but also on employees' personal characteristics. Some employees may view injustices where others may not.

4

Individual Variables and Organizational Justice

Although the effects of individual variables have received a great deal of attention in organizational literature (Tsui and O'Reilly, 1989), few studies have focused on the effects of these variables on perceptions of fairness. Taking the example of equity theory, one of the first theories of organizational justice, Major and Deaux (1982, 44) note that "what equity theory and other justice theories have generally failed to address, is the issue of individual differences in justice behavior." However, as suggested by Reis (1984, 51), "personal factors might influence perceptions of fairness not by affecting the assessed value of present outcomes and comparison levels, but rather by altering the integration of all the informational cues coming into awareness." This chapter discusses the effects of individual variables, including demographic variables, personality attributes, and cognitive processes on justice perceptions.

DEMOGRAPHIC VARIABLES AND PERCEIVED FAIRNESS

The effects of four demographic variables—gender, occupational status, organizational tenure, and level of education—on perceptions of fairness are considered.

Gender and Perceived Fairness

Research in organizational behavior (Dalton and Todor, 1985; Lyness and Thompson, 1997; Saal and Moore, 1993) suggests that the gender of an individual may influence a variety of attitudes and behaviors. For instance, Dalton and Todor, and Saal and Moore analyzed the effects of gender on justice evaluations. In a laboratory study, Saal and Moore found that gender influenced perceived fairness of promotion decisions. Female participants considered the promotion of a male participant over a female participant as unfair, while male participants considered the promotion of a female participant over a male participant as unfair. Both subjects, however, did not differ in their evaluations of the promoted participant's qualifications. Lyness and Thompson studied men and women's attitudes and behaviors in field settings. Although some similarities between the sexes were found in organizational outcomes such as compensation, in general, women tended to have less authority, few stock options, and less international mobility. In terms of organizational justice, one may imply that women are inequitably treated as compared to men. The authors note that women are more likely to be found in jobs that are not comparable to men's jobs at the same organizational level in status, power, or advancement potential.

Gender also influences justice norms. Females tend to be more inclined toward equality or even self-sacrificing patterns of reward distribution than males (Kahn, Nelson, and Gareddert, 1980). Summarizing research on gender's influences on perceptions of fairness, Major and Deaux (1982) concluded that women appeared to follow a norm of equality, whereas men appeared to follow a norm of equity. They also found that women reacted less negatively than men when they were treated unjustly by a partner. The authors suggested that women were more oriented toward the interpersonal aspects of a relationship, seeking to establish or maintain friendly relations with their partners, whereas men were more focused on the task, seeking to solve the problem, assert their status over their partners, or maximize their own gain.

Socialization across genders may explain these differences. Women are socialized to be more oriented toward help and compassion, whereas men are socialized to be more competitive. This assumption is supported by several studies (Elliot and Meeker, 1986; Lerner, 1977; Leventhal and Lane, 1970). Elliot and Meeker found that women tended to favor equality, whereas men were more likely to choose equity. They suggested that "in their youth, girls are taught to be sensitive to social relationships and to the interpersonal aspects of the situation, which fosters an emphasis on communion and cooperation; in contrast, boys are led to focus on achievement and advancement, with its concomitant stress on agency and competitiveness" (759). Lerner also noted that the "socialization of women in our society appears to lead them to be generally more inclined to evoke parity than are men" (47). Since women are socialized to be compassionate and oriented toward the satisfaction of others' needs, they are likely to prefer the equality rule of distribution compared to men.

Leventhal and Lane (1970) also noticed these gender differences in an experimental study. Their results showed that males divided reward according to the equity norm, whereas females favored the equality norm. Asked to reward themselves in a task according to their own performance, males took more than half the reward when their performance was superior to that of their partner and less than half when their performance was inferior. Females with better performance, however, attributed a significantly lower level of performance to themselves than did their male counterparts. Jackson, Gardner, and Sullivan (1992) compared male and female college graduating seniors' occupational expectations. They found that females had lower career-peak self-pay expectations than males. They also found that females had lower expectations for a career-entry pay (except for social science majors) compared to males. Concerning job performance expectations, they found that males had higher job performance expectations than females, even in occupations traditionally dominated by females. They also found that females placed more importance on interpersonal and comfort factors on the job than did males.

Sweeney and McFarlin (1997) studied gender as a moderator between distributive justice and procedural justice and organizational outcomes, such as commitment and satisfaction. Although they found that employees' intentions to stay in an organization were associated with distributive and procedural justice perceptions, perceptions of procedural justice made more of a difference for females in affecting stay intentions than it did for males. The relationship between distributive justice and satisfaction was stronger among males than females. In addition, procedural justice was a more important predictor of commitment for females than for males, whereas distributive justice was a stronger commitment for males than females. Based on these findings, one may suggest that it is not gender per se that influences justice perceptions, but gender as it is related to socialization. Women are often socialized to glean satisfaction from interactions (Kahn, O'Leary, Krulewitz, and Lamm, 1980). In work settings, other demographic variables, such as occupational status, may influence perceptions of justice.

Occupational Status and Perceived Fairness

Occupational status refers to hierarchical position within the organization. It is closely related to the employee's role in the organization. In comparing reactions of labor and management toward the fairness of distributive justice, Giacobble-Miller (1995) found that the former perceived pay as unfair, whereas the latter perceived it as fair. Lansberg (1984) studied the influence of organizational hierarchies on perceived fairness of allocation procedures. Results showed that American upper-level and middle-level managers viewed equity-based allocation of a hypothetical windfall (i.e., unexpected and one-time) pool of bonus money as more fair than equality or need-based allocations. Lower level employees from the same organizations, however, endorsed equity allocations significantly less, and equality allocations significantly more than did managers. In addition, although upper-level managers tended to support a scheme based on organization-wide equity, middle-level managers saw equity distributions within divisions of the organization as most desirable.

Justice principles, perceptions, and actions may be closely bound to the status, position, and power systems of organizations (James, 1993). In a study of 1,805 departments at 303 colleges and universities, Pfeffer and Langton (1988) found that structural factors, such as the degree of task autonomy among members, the degree of use of consensus decision making on nonpersonnel issues, the size of the department, the availability of salary information, and the tenure of the department head/chair, influence resource allocation. The authors noted that greater autonomy was associated with greater salary dispersion for the faculty. This result was further confirmed by Hardy (1990), who found that the structuring of power within different universities substantially shaped procedural choices. Universities having more centralization of power were more likely to cut departmental budgets unequally than those in which power was more decentralized.

Why would occupational status influence perceptions of fairness? Since managers often make decisions, they are likely to perceive these decisions as fair. For instance, employees in nonmanagement positions may not have access to detailed information when organizational changes are initiated and implemented. Individuals are more committed to policies that they are responsible for implementing and monitoring (Staw, 1981). It is also likely that power within organizations may influence perceptions of justice. For instance, those who have more power in organizations may have different views regarding fairness as compared to those who have less power or no power at all. Friedman and Robinson (1993) conducted a study on a sample of 237 M.B.A. students (managers) and 105 union leaders. Their results showed that among those who have less power, perceived injustice for acts perpetrated against those with whom they identify is not diminished by giving an account. They also found that union representatives were more sensitive to unjust acts than managers were. Hierarchical positions in most organizations are often related to tenure, a variable which may also influence employees' perceptions of fair treatment.

Organizational Tenure and Perceived Fairness

Organizational tenure refers to the number of years spent in a position or in an organization. Leventhal, Karuza, and Fry (1980) argued that established procedures gain greater acceptance the longer they are in use. Group members will hold more positive attitudes toward allocation procedures that ensure stability. According to the authors, such procedures increase predictability and personal security. Similarly, Lerner (1970) notes that individuals feel secure when they know what to expect; thus, they tend to support familiar ways of doing things. As people become familiar with existing procedures, they begin to accept them. However, this assumption was empirically contradicted. Beugré (1996) found a negative correlation between organizational tenure and perceptions of systemic justice. A possible explanation for this negative relationship is that employees having spent more time in an organization have the opportunity to witness several events, both bad and good. People may tend to memorize more bad events that they have experienced than good ones, at least concerning their relations with their organization. Frustrations accumulated over the years may induce a feeling of unfair treatment. The author, however, did not find negative correlations between tenure and the other justice components—distributive, procedural, and interactional justice. Further studies are needed to assess the effects (if any) of organizational tenure on justice judgments.

Level of Education and Perceived Fairness

Research on knowledge workers who are highly educated employees found that they valued freedom of action, increased responsibility, and a high degree of autonomy and control (Gillerman, 1963). Educated employees may also be more sensitive to issues of fairness since their understanding of the formal procedures, their own rights, and their willingness to influence decisions concerning their jobs may be greater than those of their less-educated counterparts. They may also have higher expectations. Failure to meet these expectations may result in disappointment and feelings of unfair treatment. Dailey and Delaney (1992) note that since skilled employees may have high job mobility, if they experience distributive and procedural inequities, they will be dissatisfied and likely to leave the organization. These authors suggest that motivation caused by perceived organizational systems' unfairness and opportunity provided by jobs available in other organizations may escalate skilled employees' intent to turn over. In other words, the existence of alternatives may render skilled workers less tolerant to unfair treatment.

Level of education is often related to competence. Ross, Thibaut, and Evenbeck (1971) considered competence to be an individual factor explaining reactions to perceived fairness. They suggest that competent individuals tend to react more negatively to a situation of unfairness than their less-competent counterparts. This assumption relies on the self-efficacy concept (Bandura, 1977, 1986), which refers to the belief that one holds regarding the extent to which he or she feels confident in performing a given task. Ross, Thibaut, and Evenbeck note that when subjects feel competent or effective rather than incompetent and ineffective, they are more likely to protest inequitable treatment. Feelings of competence raise one's hopes or expectations about the possibility of protesting effectively against an inequitable treatment.

Relational Demography and Perceptions of Fairness

Several authors (Pfeffer, 1983; Riordan and McFarlane-Shore, 1997; Tsui and O'Reilly, 1989; Wesolowski and Mossholder, 1997) suggest that considering demographic variables alone in analyzing employee attitudes and behaviors is not enough, and often may not allow us to get much information. They preferred to use the terms *organizational demography* (Pfeffer, 1983) and *relational demography* (Tsui and O'Reilly, 1989; Wesolowski and Mossholder, 1997) to describe the dispersion of demographic characteristics in a group or dyad. Relational demography refers to "comparative demographic characteristics of members of dyads or groups who are in a position to engage in regular interactions" (Tsui and O'Reilly, 1989, 403).

Wesolowski and Mossholder (1997) conducted an empirical study to analyze the effects of relational demography on people's perceptions of fairness in dyadic relationships. They used four demographic variables: age, gender, level of education, and race. They found that subordinates in mixed-race dyads exhibited lower mean satisfaction and perceived less procedural justice compared to those in same-race dyads. These findings showed the importance of relational demography in assessing justice perceptions, and call for more empirical investigations. Perhaps, when superior and supervisor are of different races, disagreement which would have been easily solved may become more salient. Also, superiors may tend to be more supportive of same-race subordinates than different-race subordinates. In an era where diversity in the workplace is an important concern both for organizational scholars and managers, researchers should give a great deal of attention to the study of the influence of relational demography on subordinates' perceptions of fairness. In addition to demographic variables, personality variables are likely to influence justice perceptions. Reviewing all of them is beyond the scope of this book; therefore, I will focus on two of them: negative affectivity (NA) and hostile attribution bias (HAB).

PERSONALITY VARIABLES AND PERCEIVED FAIRNESS

Negative Affectivity and Perceived Fairness

"Negative affect is a general dimension of subjective stress and unpleasurable engagement that subsumes a variety of aversive moods, including anger, contempt, disgust, guilt, and nervousness with low negative affectivity being a state of calmness and serenity" (Watson, Clark, and Tellegen, 1988, 1063). Negative affectivity measures reflect an individual's disposition to respond negatively regardless of the situation (Folger and Konovsky, 1989). High negative affectivity individuals tend to be distressed, agitated, pessimistic, and dissatisfied (Levin and Stokes, 1989). Watson and Clark (1984, 483) contend that "high negative affectivity individuals are more likely to report distress, discomfort, and dissatisfaction over time and regardless of the situation, even in the absence of any overt or objective source of distress." According to the authors, such individuals tend to focus more on the negative aspects of the world in general. In contrast, low negative affectivity individuals appear to be more satisfied, self-secure, and calm, and focus less on and are more resilient in response to life's daily frustrations and irritations. Positive affect, however, refers to the extent to which a person feels enthusiastic, active, and alert (Watson, Clark, and Tellengen, 1988).

No matter the situation, individuals high on negative affectivity will perceive injustices where others may see justice. Bazerman (1993, 199) contends that "in many organizational environments, individuals will perceive unfairness no matter what decisions are made by the manager or organization." Ball, Trevino, and Sims (1993) studied the effects of negative affectivity on reactions to organizational punishment. They found that high negative affectivity subordinates perceived significantly more negative demeanor, arbitrariness, harshness, and less explanation in the punishment administered. They also viewed the punishment as less distributively and procedurally fair, were less trusting of and less satisfied with the supervisor who administered the punishment, and expressed less organizational commitment and higher turnover intentions. High negative affectivity individuals may also tend to attribute hostile intentions to others.

Hostile Attributional Bias and Perceived Fairness

According to Dodge (1980) and Dodge, Price, Bachorowski, and Newman (1990), hostile attributional bias refers to the tendency to explain ambiguous situations by hostile intentions from their perpetrator. The authors found that children with hostile attributional tendencies are likely to express behavioral difficulties in interacting with peers. In organizational settings, one may suggest that hostile attributional bias would lead employees to perceive bad intentions in their supervisor's behavior. Instead of viewing the situation objectively, they will tend to convince themselves that their supervisor is against their self-interests. To the extent that such intentions are attributed to the harmdoer, the victim is likely to feel unfairly treated and perhaps display aggressive behaviors. To the extent that the individual perceives that the others have hostile intentions, he or she will feel unfairly treated. However, there are few empirical studies that support such a claim. Baron, Neuman, and Geddes (1997) contend that when individuals conclude that they have been treated unfairly, they consider such treatment as stemming from malevolent intentions on the part of others. The authors also note that perceptions on the part of individuals that they have been treated unfairly may be closely linked in the minds of such persons, with attributions of hostile intent to the perceived sources of such injustices.

Other personality variables which may influence perceptions of fairness are: belief in a just world (Lerner, 1975; Ball, Trevino, and Sims, 1994), Type A behavior pattern (Baron, Neuman, and Geddes, 1997), and the Protestant work ethic (Greenberg, 1977; Kidron, 1978). "Protestant work ethic refers to a commitment to the values of hard work, to work itself as an objective, and to the work organization as an inevitable structure within which those internalized values can be satisfied" (Kidron, 1978, 240). In a field study on observers' reactions to punishments, Ball, Trevino, and Sims (1994) found that individuals with a strong belief in a just world saw punishment as more constructive and as providing more control than those with a weak belief in a just world. They also viewed the punishment as less harsh. According to Rubin and Peplau (1975, 71), "high believers in a just world will derogate victims even when there is no reason to think that the victim was in fact responsible of his or her misfortune." Since justice is a perceptual phenomenon, it is important to analyze the impact of cognitive variables on perceptions of fairness. How people interpret events may shape their perceptions of fair treatment.

COGNITIONS AND ORGANIZATIONAL JUSTICE

The Role of Perceptions in Justice Judgments

In studying justice, what is important is not reality itself, but the subject's perceptions of reality. For example, an employee's perceptions of criticism emanating from his or her supervisor influences his or her own reactions. Perceived justice is an evaluative judgment about the rightness of a person's fate or treatment by others (Furby, 1986). The value attached to an outcome may also influence justice evaluations. If the outcome is relevant to the person, failure to get it may raise greater feelings of injustice. Individuals with high expectancies may be more dissatisfied with a given outcome than those with lower expectancies (Major and Deaux, 1982). Brockner, Tyler, and Cooper-Schneider (1992, 258) conducted two studies to analyze the effect of prior commitment on individuals' reactions to perceived fairness (or unfairness). The first study analyzed reactions of layoff survivors, and the second explored citizens' commitment to legal authorities. They concluded that "individuals who had high hopes for how they would be treated by the institution, as reflected by their prior commitment to the institution, were much more likely to react negatively in the face of unfair treatment, relative to those with lower hopes and expectations." The authors explained their results by suggesting an *expectancy-violation effect*; that is, people react more strongly to another party's actions that violate their previous expectations of how the other party is likely to behave. The expectation-violation effect is similar to the concept of *entitlement* (Rousseau, 1989), which postulates that over time, people develop feelings of entitlement, meaning perceived obligations that their employers have toward them. Failure to fit these obligations may lead to perceptions of unfair treatment and thereby great deceptions.

What is just or unjust is determined by the individual, but may also depend on his or her interpretations of the causes of the events. According to Stroesser and Heuer (1996, 726) "a cognitive bias alone can make individuals see unfair treatment even where it does not exist, independent of motivational concerns." They contend that cognitive biases, such as the tendency to form illusory correlations between two distinct variables, may intervene to create inaccurate perceptions of differential treatment. The authors also state that illusory correlations refer to misperceptions of the relationship between group membership and the desirability of behaviors performed by group members. Justice also may depend on the types of the attributions made by the perceiver.

Causal Attributions and Justice Evaluations

Stepina and Perrewe (1991) contend that once people develop feelings of equity (or inequity), they tend to retain these feelings over time. Such stable feelings may influence justice judgments. Specifically, people may tend to consider their own actions as fairer than those of others. For instance, people who tend to attribute their success to external factors and their failure to internal factors may allocate rewards equally when they are the superior performers and equitably when they are the inferior performers (Major and Deaux, 1982). The type of attributions people make after a negative outcome may influence their subsequent reactions. Lind (1997) notes that people are less likely to sue their former employers when they attribute the causes of their termination to external factors, such as a downturn in the economy, than to internal factors.

Social comparison may also be an important source of information on which people rely to interpret workplace injustice (Greenberg and Alge, in press). If a person is unfairly treated and perceived that others received the same treatment, he or she may temper his or her reactions. After all, others also share one's "plight." However, if the individual perceives that he or she is the only victim of injustice, he or she may react more aggressively.

Cohen (1982, 125) notes that perceptions of justice are based fundamentally on attributions of cause and responsibility: "Potential injustices become actual injustices to the person only if and when the discrepancy between actual and deserved outcomes is attributed to something other than the actor's own behavior." The author also contends that people are more resentful when someone deprives them intentionally than when the cause of the person's action is attributed externally. In a field study, Sweeney, McFarlin, and Cotton (1991) found that internals who perceived that their job allowed them the opportunity to influence a decision process had higher ratings of procedural justice than did internals who did not perceive such influence. In addition, internals who experienced high perceived influence gave higher ratings of procedural justice than did externals who also had high perceived influence. Kidd and Utne (1978) consider that inequity reduction is affected by the subject's locus of causation of the inequity, its stability, intentionality, and controllability.

Self-Serving Bias and Perceptions of Fairness

Self-serving bias refers to a tendency to attribute desirable outcomes to internal causes, but undesirable ones to external factors, leading people to credit themselves for positive results, but blame others for negative ones (Baron, 1993). According to Bradley (1978, 68), "people tend to accept responsibility for positive behavioral outcomes and deny responsibility for negative behavioral outcomes." The author identifies four conditions leading to these types of attributions:

1. when an individual's performance is public;
2. when an individual perceives himself or herself to have higher choice in taking an action and, as a result, feels responsible for the outcomes of his or her actions;
3. under conditions designed to produce high ego involvement; and
4. under conditions designed to produce high objective self-awareness.

Self-serving bias may influence people's perceptions of fairness (Greenberg, 1981, 1983; Tornblom, 1977). Greenberg (1983) found that respondents tended to consider as fair, gasoline allocation plans that were believed to have the least negative effect on themselves. In a study related to employee attitudes toward parental leave policies, Grover (1991) found that respondents who were planning to bear children or who intended to take leave considered these policies fair, compared to those who did not. Similarly, Grienberger, Rutte, and Van Knippenberg (1997) conducted an experimental study related to people's perceptions of fairness concerning outcomes and procedures and those of comparison others. They found that when participants received the more favorable treatment or procedure (being allowed to choose their performance task), they did not seem to focus on differences in treatment between themselves and the comparison others. However, they tended to focus on these differences when their outcomes and procedures were perceived as unfair. These findings support Tornblom's (1977) assumption that people are more likely to favor policies that benefit them.

Although recent studies (Baron, Neuman, and Geddes, 1997; Folger and Baron, 1996; Greenberg and Alge, in press) contend that people react aggressively when they feel unfairly treated, it is unlikely that they would react so when they witness injustices. People are more sensitive to injustices involving themselves than others (Tornblom, 1977). In addition, people may tend to judge their own actions as fairer compared to those of others. Greenberg (1983) found that participants rated overpayments to themselves as being less unfair than overpayments to others, and underpayment to themselves as being more unfair than underpayment to others. However, this egocentric bias was eliminated by the induction of self-awareness. Self-aware participants rated overpayment and underpayment to themselves and to others as being equally unfair. Diekman (1997, 4) notes that "since people are self-interested, they will often take more than an equal share, particularly when they perceive it socially acceptable and fair to do so and/or when they believe they can get away with it." People may seek more justice for themselves than for others.

This chapter has discussed the effects of individual variables on perceptions of justice. Despite their importance in justice perceptions, individual variables alone do not fully explain how people interpret the fairness of several events. The way employees are treated by management, and the conditions in which they perform their daily tasks matter, too.

5

Organizational Factors and Organizational Justice

Several organizational factors influence employee perceptions of fairness. Analyzing all of them would be a tedious task, and beyond the scope of this book. Therefore, this chapter will focus on organizational factors considered as potential triggers of justice judgments. Such factors include: organizational change, leader behavior, performance appraisal, punishment, pay, employee selection, and organizational culture.

ORGANIZATIONAL CHANGE

Recent changes, such as downsizing, reengineering, and restructuring, occurring in the workplace may influence employees' perceptions of fairness. Beugré (1997) conducted a field study analyzing the impact of organizational changes on perceived fairness, and identified three types of changes: cost-cutting, structural, and role-reduction. Cost-cutting changes were changes whose main purpose was to cut operating costs, such as downsizing, layoffs, budget cuts, and pay cuts. Structural changes were designed to change processes and structures within the organization, such as technological change, increased diversity in the workplace, change in management, restructuring, and reengineering. Finally, role-reduction changes were designed to reduce employee responsibility and power, and included use of computers to monitor employee performance, increased use of part-time workers, and job sharing. I used this classification to analyze the relationship between organizational changes and perceptions of justice.

Cost-Cutting Changes and Perceptions of Justice

Several authors (Cobb, Wooten, and Folger, 1995; Daly, 1995; Daly and Geyer, 1994; Kozlowski, Chao, Smith, and Hedlund, 1993; Novelli, Kirkman, and Shapiro, 1995) have attempted to consider justice as an important component in implementing organizational changes. For instance, although downsizing may help to increase organizational effectiveness (Kozlowski et al., 1993), it is likely to raise negative feelings among employees. Novelli, Kirkman, and Shapiro (1995) note that effective change is not simply a matter of clearly articulating an energizing vision and getting people to 'buy in' to the desired outcome of the change; it is crucial to focus on the justice aspects of the change process. These authors contend that if employees are fairly treated during a change program, they may be likely to accept it and contribute to its successful implementation. However, when they are unfairly treated, they may resist the changes and withhold effort to implement them. Daly and Geyer (1994) analyzed the perceived fairness of relocation decisions. Contrary to Folger (1977), they found that the opportunity to voice one's opinion did not show any effect on procedural fairness. The authors explained their findings by relying on what they called "employees' prior expectations." When employees do not expect voice to occur, the absence of voice is not perceived as unfair. However, Daly (1995, 416) suggests that "the process of explaining decisions in a change context helps employees to adapt to the change because the lack of an explanation is often regarded by employees as unfair, generating resentment toward management and toward the decision."

Brockner, DeWitt, Grover, and Reed (1987) and Brockner, Tyler, and Cooper-Schneider (1992) conducted a series of studies on the impact of layoffs on survivors. They found that witnessing layoffs may have an important influence on survivors' state of mind and commitment to the organization. Brockner et al. (1987) found that survivors of actual layoffs in a chain of retail stores reported feeling more committed to their organization when they believed that the victims were adequately compensated. This result was further confirmed in several studies (Brockner et al., 1994; Brockner and Greenberg, 1990; Konovsky and Brockner, 1993). Besides layoffs, several other factors may influence survivors' reactions. Frequency of the layoffs and the psychological distance between laid-off employees and survivors, and outcome negativity are such moderators. Brockner and Greenberg (1990) suggested that survivors were likely to view a layoff as more negative when it was expected to recur, and when they felt attached to the layoff victims. Konovsky and Brockner (1993) also found that survivors reacted negatively when outcome negativity was high and interpersonal justice was low; and experienced resentment toward the employing organization and its management. The negativity of an outcome may raise concerns not only for distributive justice, but also for procedural justice. Greenberg (1990b) notes that individuals are likely to raise concerns of procedural justice when they receive negative rather than positive outcomes.

Structural Changes and Perceptions of Justice

Other organizational changes such as implementation of affirmative action policies leading to workplace diversity may result in feelings of unfair treatment. To the extent that increased diversity leads to contact between persons from sharply contrasting ethnic backgrounds (Baron and Neuman, 1996), it may raise concerns for justice. Frequent interactions raise problems of communication and trust. Jackson, Stone, and Alvarez (1992, 80–81) note that "diversity makes social identities more salient, which in turn causes personal identity to be submerged, reduces interpersonal attraction among dissimilar team members, increases anxiety, and triggers stereotyping and biased information processing." They found that workplace diversity is due in part to affirmative action policies. Despite its positive intentions (allowing equal opportunity for all workers, especially women and minorities), affirmative action can raise concerns for justice (or injustice). According to Heilman (1994, 155):

Feeling of being cheated out of deserved organizational rewards resulting from affirmative action is likely to influence attitudes toward the individual believed to have benefited from one's loss, and attitudes toward the work setting itself . . . Essential to the feeling of being cheated is the experience of injustice and outrage at having been treated unfairly, of having been denied what is deserved.

The level of perceived injustice was directly related to the discrepancy in merits between the successful minority candidate; and the provision of either an ethical or legislative justification for the selection decisions further exacerbated feelings of injustice. Leck, Saunders, and Charbonneau (1996) found that when affirmative action policies are perceived as fair, employees tend to develop positive reactions. However, they are likely to resist integration (of newcomers) when they perceived that notions of equity were violated (distributive justice) and employment-related decisions were inconsistently applied (procedural justice). Parker, Bales, and Christiansen (1997) conducted an empirical study on a sample of 7,228 federal employees. They found that white males as well as white females, and ethnic minority respondents perceived an organization supporting affirmative action as fair. This surprising result concerning specifically white males may be explained by the high level of education of the sample. More than 80 percent of the employees who participated in the study had a bachelor's degree or more. In addition, the authors collected their data in 1989, a period when affirmative action might not have the political and emotional connotations of the 1990s.

Role-Reduction Changes and Perceptions of Justice

Organizational changes, such as the use of electronic devices to monitor employee performance, job sharing, or the use of part-time employees, tend to reduce employee power and role. Therefore, they are likely to raise concerns for distributive justice as well as procedural justice. Kidwell and Bennett (1994) studied employee reactions to electronic control systems. They found that employee perceptions of procedural fairness were important antecedents of attitudinal responses related to the use of electronic control system technologies to monitor performance. They also found that employees considered the system to be fairer when it collected accurate information consistently and in an unbiased manner. The flexibility of the system to correct mistakes was also an important factor in enhancing employees' perceptions of fairness. Finally, the authors found that an important factor in achieving fairness was employees' beliefs that the electronic control system did not collect private information that was unrelated to job performance.

Despite the apparent negative influence of organizational changes on perceptions of fairness, one may suggest that it is not changes per se that lead to perceptions of unfairness, but the way employees are treated during the implementation of specific changes. When employees welcome changes and are well treated during their implementation, they may be likely to perceive justice. However, when employees feel unfairly treated during the implementation of a change process, they would be likely to resist it. Cooper and Markus (1995) note that people resist change not because they want to, but because of the way they are treated during the implementation of the change process. An important organizational factor influencing the implementation of changes is leader behavior.

LEADER BEHAVIOR

Although leadership has received a great deal of research attention in organizational behavior and industrial/organizational psychology, few studies have concerned its impact on employee perceptions of fairness. Meindl (1989) notes that organizational scholars have often neglected issues of distributive justice and how the preferred allocation rules are associated with leadership variables. Lind and Tyler (1988) and Tyler and Bies (1990) contend that leaders' enactment of procedures influence subordinates' perceptions of fairness. McFarlin and Sweeney (1992) found that subordinates who perceived reward allocations and procedures to be unfair tended to give low ratings to their supervisors. These low ratings may be interpreted as expressions of negative feelings toward the supervisor following perceptions of unfair treatment. Meindl (1989) studied the leadership style of several managers in relation to perceived fairness. Results showed that high task-oriented leaders preferred equity-based allocation rules. They were likely to distribute rewards on the basis of individual performance. Tyler and Caine (1981) also found a relationship between leader behavior and perceived fairness. They conducted both experimental and field studies. Their results showed that in natural settings, individuals tended to focus on procedures, whereas in experimental situations, they tended to consider the outcomes in evaluating a leader's fairness. Tyler, Rasinski, and Spodick (1985, 76) suggested that "when team leaders showed strong consideration of members' input, team members saw the process as fairer, and consequently, had greater commitment to the decision, greater attachment to the team, and greater trust in the leader." Studying the effects of authorities' behavior on subordinates' justice evaluations, Tyler (1994) argues that if authorities are regarded as trustworthy, then people are willing to judge their outcomes to be fair.

Leader fairness influences subordinates' attitudes and organizational citizenship behavior (Deluga, 1994). When leaders are perceived as fair, employees tend to engage in organizational citizenship behavior. If organizations are considered as social contracts (Keeley, 1988), a person's sense of fairness in the social contract would depend very much on a leader's behavior (Farh, Podsakoff, and Organ, 1990). Leaders' fairness is particularly important in evaluating subordinates' performance. Lack of fair treatment from leaders may alter the psychological contract between employees and employers (Rousseau, 1989, 1995). Cobb and Frey (1996) studied the influence of leader fairness on supervisor-subordinate relations. Procedurally fair leadership was operationalized by the extent to which supervisors enacted three specific behaviors: facilitation of voice, accuracy, and adherence to formal policy and procedures. Their results showed that subordinates were more satisfied and committed to procedurally fair leaders. In addition, subordinates chose to remain with the supervisor who enacted procedurally fair behavior and leave the supervisor who did not, regardless of the supervisor's performance assessment itself and the pay outcome associated with it. Cobb and Frey also found that when leaders acted unfairly, their decisions were seen as unfair even when subordinates benefitted from them. In addition, leaders play both instrumental and symbolic roles in the delivery of justice that become even more important to their subordinates in times of change (Cobb, Wooten, and Folger, 1995). Lind, Tyler, and Huo (1997) note that when people are dealing with superordinate authorities, inferences about the benevolence of those authorities is a key antecedent to procedural justice reaction. An area where a leader influences his or her subordinate's reactions is how fairly the subordinate's performance is evaluated.

PERFORMANCE APPRAISAL

Several organizational scholars (Folger, Konovski, and Cropanzano, 1992; Greenberg, 1986a, 1986b; Taylor, Tracy, Renard, Harrison, and Carroll, 1995) have studied the relationship between performance appraisal and fairness. When procedures used to measure employee performance are consistent across situations, employees tend to perceive them as fair. Greenberg (1986a) identified consistent application of standards across people as a key determinant of procedural fairness in performance evaluations. He identified five procedural components: soliciting input prior to the evaluation and using it, having a two-way communication during interview, having the ability to challenge/rebut evaluation, rater familiarity with ratee's work, and consistent application of standards related to the fairness of performance evaluation. To the extent that these measures are followed, an evaluation is likely to be perceived as fair.

Landy, Barnes, and Murphy (1978) studied the relationship between fairness and performance evaluations in a field study. They found that performance evaluation is perceived as fair and accurate when supervisors evaluate performance frequently, are familiar with the performance levels of the person, are in agreement with the subordinate's on-job duties, and engage in helping the subordinate to eliminate performance weaknesses. These results were further corroborated by Landy, Barnes-Farrell, and Cleveland (1980) in a follow-up study. Lissak (1983) found a positive association between procedures and performance evaluation; participants having an input into their performance evaluation procedure considered it fairer than those who did not.

Folger and Greenberg (1985) suggest that there is a general tendency for fair procedures to engender greater outcome acceptance than unfair procedures. Folger, Konovsky, and Cropanzano (1992) developed a due process model of performance, implying that employees should not only be told about the appraisal rating itself, but also how the rating was derived. Folger and Lewis (1993) suggest that self-appraisal is likely to increase the perceived fairness of performance appraisal techniques by allowing the employee to provide valuable information about his or her job and how it is done. When employees have an input in the performance evaluation process, they tend to consider it fair.

PUNISHMENT

Punishment is subsequent to certain behaviors referred to as "misconduct." A misconduct is a behavior that falls short of the agent's moral or technical (work) standard (Trevino, 1992). According to Trevino (1992, 1479), "punishment refers to the application of a negative consequence or the withdrawal of a positive consequence from someone under one's control or supervision." Butterfield, Trevino, and Ball (1996) referred to punishment as a supervisor's application of a negative consequence following a subordinate's undesirable behavior, with the intention of decreasing the frequency of that behavior. When such behavior is displayed, the manager is likely to punish the subordinate.

But how is this action perceived, not only by the "victim" (the punished), but also by those who witness it (observers)? For the victim, punishment may produce anger and resentment directed toward the *punisher*. In most organizations, punishment goes beyond the dyad superior/subordinate and encompasses those who witness it. If a punishment is perceived as unfair by observers, the superior may lose their confidence, and because of this perceived injustice, his or her authority may suffer. Ball, Trevino, and Sims (1994) found that subordinates reacted more positively to a punishment which they perceived to be fair. Butterfield, Trevino, and Ball (1996) studied punishment from managers' point of view. They found that in contrast to subordinates' tendency to focus on issues of distributive justice, managers' own fairness concerns tended to focus on procedural issues, such as whether organizational policies and procedures were followed. They also found that managers were frequently aware of and concerned about feelings of fair treatment expressed by punished subordinates, their work groups, and their larger organization.

In addition to punishment as negative outcome, procedures underlying it may be questioned. Are they fair? Did the victim receive a due process? Observers may evaluate the punishment outcome as fair if the punishment process is viewed as fair (Leventhal, 1976). In such a situation, the negativity of the outcome is offset by the fairness of the procedures. Trevino (1992, 659) suggests that "group members are concerned about whether punishment procedures are aligned with fundamental group values and norms and whether these procedures are neutrally applied." In administering punishment in organizations, managers should apply the "hot stove rule," that is, discipline should be immediate, impersonal, and consistent. Punishments are perceived as fairer when they are private and delivered in a timely manner (Arvey and Jones, 1985). Although punishment is a negative outcome, some authors (Arvey and Jones, 1985; O'Reilly and Puffer, 1989) note that its fairness bears some positive consequences for employees and organizations. Arvey and Jones found that fairness of punishment increases observer's performance. After all, if rules are enacted, sanctions should be applied when these rules are violated. Failure to do so, may give "free ride" to opportunistic individuals. Enforcing existing rules may imply that honest employees will not be victims of opportunistic colleagues. O'Reilly and Puffer found that deserved punishment positively influences observers' motivation, satisfaction, and perceptions of equity.

PAY SYSTEMS

If there is one organizational system raising concerns for justice, it is the distribution of outcomes. The fairness of what employees get is important, and influences their evaluation of the organization. Pay systems may raise concerns for distributive justice as well as procedural justice. Lawler (1971) conceived that employees considered their pay as equitable when it was proportional to their inputs. But consideration of procedural matters may suggest that a pay system which allows participation and inputs from the employee will be perceived as fairer than one that does not. What one gets is just as important as how one gets it. Equity theory deals with the fairness of outcomes. Does an employee get a fair pay for a fair day of work? Is this outcome proportional to the inputs? Is it fair compared to that received by comparison others? Such questions have been addressed by equity theory (Adams, 1965; Walster, Walster, and Berscheid, 1978). In organizations, employees are concerned by the fairness of the outcomes they get.

Pay systems may also raise concerns for procedural justice. Specific forms of compensation such as an open pay system, influence employee perceptions of procedural fairness. According to Folger and Greenberg (1985), an open pay system refers to a compensation system in which employees are given access to information about various individuals' pay levels. The authors note that "although open pay systems do not give workers any voice in how their pay will be determined, they provide information about how others will make these decisions and provide important assurances that these procedures are not being violated" (163). For this reason, they are likely to enhance perceptions of justice. Folger and Greenberg suggest that the very transparency of the open pay system discourages abuse and favoritism, thereby promoting procedural fairness based on consistency and bias suppression. Secrecy of a pay system may raise suspicion concerning the fairness of the outcome itself and the fairness of the procedures underlining it. Although employees may not receive detailed information about their colleagues' outcomes, they should have some knowledge about the procedures determining outcomes in their organization. Such knowledge, however imperfect, may influence their perceptions of justice.

Another type of pay system which may influence employees' perceptions of fairness is the cafeteria-style benefit plans, which allow employees to determine the relative mix of their fringe benefits and wage package and may increase perceptions of procedural justice as well as distributive justice. "Allowing people to choose what benefits they want increases their chances of receiving highly desired outcomes, relative to a system in which the employer makes the choice for all employees" (Folger and Greenberg, 1985, 165). To the extent that employees participate in determining the level of their outcomes, they may find these outcomes fair.

EMPLOYEE SELECTION

Research on justice issues in hiring (Bies and Moag, 1986; Folger and Greenberg, 1985; Gilliland, 1993) suggests that fair treatment during the hiring process influences job applicants' perceptions of fairness. For Gilliland (1993), this attitude goes beyond the hiring process and invades the candidate's subsequent behaviors once he or she is hired. Development of attitudes such as trust, honesty, commitment, and citizenship behaviors will depend on how one was treated during the hiring process. It is therefore important for organizations to develop and implement fair hiring procedures. For instance, an employee who was fairly treated during the hiring process may have a first impression of fairness of his or her new organization. This first impression may serve as a reference to judge further treatments within the organization. A job interview often represents the first contact an applicant has with a prospective employer.

Bies and Moag (1986) have studied the fairness of interpersonal treatment during recruitment interviews. Applicants who felt treated with respect and dignity perceived recruitment procedures as fairer than those who felt treated in a condescending manner. Reactions to selection procedures may influence the ability of an organization to attract and hire highly qualified applicants (Boudreaux and Rynes, 1985; Murphy, 1986). Robertson and Smith (1989) note that the perceived fairness of selection testing may influence the efficacy and self-esteem of rejected applicants. "From a legal perspective, the perceived fairness of the selection procedure may influence applicants' decisions to pursue discrimination cases" (Gilliland, 1993, 695).

Recruitment procedures may raise concerns for: distributive fairness (getting the job); procedural justice (conduct of formal interviews, feedback on interviews); interactional justice (treatment during the interview); and systemic justice (fairness of the recruitment process). Gililland (1993) developed a model of recruitment fairness, identifying three distribution elements: equity, equality, and needs, as well as three procedural elements: formal characteristics (job relatedness, opportunity to perform, reconsideration opportunity, consistency of administration), explanation (feedback, selection information, and honesty), and interpersonal treatment (interpersonal treatment of administrator, two-way communication, and property of questions). I expand this model to include interactional justice and systemic justice concerning the selection process (see Table 1). What Gilliland named formal characteristics, is part of procedural justice, whereas the explanation and interpersonal treatment elements are components of interactional justice. The combination of distributive, procedural, and interactional justice may lead to a judgment related to the fairness of the selection process as a whole (systemic justice). Gilliland argues that perceptions of distributive, procedural, and interactional justice are combined to form an overall evaluation of the fairness of the selection system (systemic justice). Schuler (1993) suggested four factors influencing the perceived acceptability of selection situations:

a. the presence of job-relevant information that can aid job acceptance decisions;

b. participation or representation in the development of the selection process;

c. understanding of the evaluation process and the task-relevance of the selection procedures; and

d. content and form of feedback.

Table 1
Employee Selection and Perceptions of Fairness

Distributive Justice	Procedural Justice	Interactional Justice	Systemic Justice
Hiring	Job related questions	Interpersonal treatment	Fairness of the selection process
Rejection	Opportunity to perform	Two-way communication	
	Reconsideration opportunity	Property of questions	General impression of the organization as fair
	Consistency of administration	Honesty/integrity of interviewer	
	Existence of feedback mechanisms	Proper greetings	
	Information about selection procedures		

A specific procedure raising concerns for fairness is the requirement of drug testing. Not only are such tests considered as invading the privacy of prospective job applicants, but their validity and job relevance aspects are often questioned. Konovsky and Cropanzano (1993) state that if such tests are part of a selection procedure, applicants should be notified in advance. They noted that participants considered drug testing fair when there was advance notification. Whatever the fairness of hiring procedures, they often symbolize the dominant culture of an organization.

ORGANIZATIONAL CULTURE

"An organization's policies and culture greatly influence the way individuals are treated and their perceptions of fairness" (O'Leary-Kelly, Griffin, and Glew, 1996, 243). The culture prevailing in an organization may influence perceptions of fairness. Mannix, Neale, and Northcraft (1995) studied the impact of organizational culture on allocation rules. They identified three distributive rules: equity, equality, and need. They also considered three types of organizational cultures: economically-oriented, relationship-oriented, and personal development-oriented. They found that group members in economically-oriented cultures reported using an equity allocation rule, those in relationship-oriented cultures were likely to use equality rule, and those in personal development-oriented cultures, a need allocation rule.

Relations in organizations may be described as cooperative relations within which economic productivity is a primary goal. According to Kabanoff (1991), in such relations, equity rather than equality tends to be the chief principle of distributive justice. The author notes that the dominant distributive value within an economically directed relationship tends to be equity, and the cognitive, motivational, and moral orientations of the parties in the relationship are congruent with this emphasis on differentiating between each other in terms of inputs and outcomes. In relations in which the fostering or maintenance of enjoyable social relations is the common goal, equality tends to be the dominant distributive principle. Equality implies that the different members of a relationship have equal value as individuals, which creates the optimum conditions for the maintenance of mutual self-esteem. Equality of outcomes emphasizes members' *common fate*, thus promoting solidarity (Kabanoff, 1991). Similarly, Meindl (1989) found that equity was the preferred principle when productivity was emphasized, and equality was chosen when solidarity was the goal sought by the allocator.

In this chapter, I have analyzed the organizational determinants of justice. It is now important to discuss the attitudinal and behavioral consequences following employees' perceptions of justice (or injustice).

6

Employee Reactions to Organizational Justice

In chapters 4 and 5, I have discussed individual characteristics and organizational factors influencing perceptions of justice. In this chapter, I focus on how people react to perceptions of fairness (or unfairness). By so doing, I have relied on the rich body of empirical and theoretical research that has discussed employee reactions to perceived fairness. The relationships between perceived fairness and attitudinal outcomes (job satisfaction, trust, organizational commitment) and behavioral outcomes (organizational citizenship behavior, turnover, theft, workplace aggression) are discussed. Although this list is certainly not exhaustive, it depicts a general picture of employee attitudes and behaviors engendered by perceptions of justice.

JOB SATISFACTION

Job satisfaction refers to a set of affective reactions employees hold for their job. Perceptions of fairness tend to influence employee satisfaction with various facets of their job. In a field study conducted on a sample of 365 managers, Summers and Hendrix (1991) found that perceived pay equity had a direct effect on job satisfaction. In another field study, Folger and Konovsky (1989) found that perceptions of both distributive and procedural justice led to outcome satisfaction. According to Lind and Tyler (1988), satisfaction is one of the principal consequences of procedural fairness. Earlier findings by Alexander and Ruderman (1987) contend that procedural justice positively influences job satisfaction. Fryxell and Gordon (1989) found that the amounts of procedural and distributive justice afforded by a grievance system were the strongest predictors of satisfaction with a union.

In a study of the Canadian Air Force, Lissak (1983) found that procedural justice contributed more to job satisfaction than distributive justice. Such a relationship between procedural justice and satisfaction was found by Thibaut and Walker (1975), who compared the adversarial legal procedure (employed in the United States and the United Kingdom) and the inquisitorial system (employed in continental Europe). They found that satisfaction was higher under the first system (allowing more participation to the litigants) than under the second one. "Increased procedural justice in organizations is more likely to affect the display of discrete behaviors reflecting loyalty and commitment to the organization than ongoing, day-to-day job performance" (Taylor et al., 1995, 519). Manogran, Stauffer, and Conlon (1994) found that distributive justice and procedural justice had a significant direct positive effect on job satisfaction and commitment.

TRUST

Trust is essential for stable social relationships (Blau, 1964). This is particularly true in organizational settings, where different people with various backgrounds come together to work toward a common purpose. Trust refers to an expectancy held by an individual or a group that the word, promise, verbal or written statement of another individual or group may be relied upon (Zand, 1972; Zucker, 1986; Dasgupta, 1988; Bromiley and Cummings, 1995; Mayer, Davis, and Schoorman, 1995; McAllister, 1995; Chiles and McMackin, 1996). Implicit in this definition of trust are the concepts of vulnerability and dependency. Trust refers also to the willingness of a party to be vulnerable to the actions of another party based on the expectation that the other will perform a particular action important to the trustor, irrespective of the ability to monitor or control that other party (Zand, 1972; Mayer, Davis, and Schoorman, 1995; Chiles and McMackin,

1996). McAllister (1995) identified two types of trust: affect and cognition-based. Affect-based trust refers to emotional bonds between individuals, whereas cognition-based trust refers to trust based on competence and responsibility.

The level of an employee's affect-based trust in a supervisor may be positively related to procedural and interactional justice. Tyler and Degoey (1995, 403) emphasized the impact of procedural justice on trust by suggesting that "procedures that are structurally and interactionally fair will engender trust in the system and in the implementers of decisions, whereas a lack of structural and/or interactional fairness will elicit low levels of trust." In an empirical study, Konovsky and Pugh (1993) found a strong correlation between subordinates' perceptions of their supervisor's procedural treatment and trust in the supervisor. Creed and Douglas (1995, 20) found that managers' beliefs and actions directly and indirectly influence trust in organizations: "Managers' overall attitudes and behaviors determine the initial levels of trust expectations within the organization, in effect enacting the context within which organizational processes will be embedded."

Butler (1991) identified ten conditions of trust: availability, competence, consistency, fairness, integrity, loyalty, openness, overall trust, promise fulfillment, and receptivity. Fairness is considered one of the ten conditions leading to trust. When supervisors are perceived as fair and unbiased, they are likely to be trusted by their subordinates. "Beliefs in the integrity, loyalty, and promise fulfillment of decision makers might reflect beliefs that an organization will continue in the future to provide the need and value fulfillments required for job satisfaction" (666). Kim and Mauborgne (1995) argue that one may build trust through procedural justice. Listening to employees and taking into account their concerns may help build trust between managers and their employees. "Managers need to involve their subordinates in making decisions, and give them a chance of appealing if they think those decisions are wrong" (61). For Brockner and Siegel (1995), unfair procedures lead people to believe they cannot trust that they will receive distributive justice over the longer term. Beugré (1996, 1997) found a positive relationship between organizational justice and trust. The four justice dimensions (distributive, procedural, interactional, and systemic justice) identified by the author positively predicted trust. When people feel fairly treated, they tend to trust the organization and its managers. Perceptions of fairness also enhance organizational commitment.

ORGANIZATIONAL COMMITMENT

Commitment is the strength of an individual's identification with involvement in a particular organization (Porter, Steers, Mowday, and Boulian, 1974; Mowday, Steers, and Porter, 1979). This definition contains three aspects:

1. a belief in and acceptance of organizational goals and values;
2. a willingness to exert effort towards organizational goal accomplishment; and
3. a strong desire to maintain organizational membership.

This also includes an affective component which refers to an emotional bond between the individual and the organization (e.g., Meyer and Allen, 1984, 1991; Meyer, Allen, and Smith, 1993). Becker (1960) developed an instrumental view of organizational commitment, which consists of following some patterns of behavior because of the perceived costs of doing otherwise. It is more instrumental than just an affective link between the employee and his or her organization. Several authors (e.g., Mowday, Porter, and Steers, 1982; Reichers, 1986; Allen and Meyer; 1990; Meyer, Allen, and Smith, 1993) considered organizational commitment as a multidimensional construct. Recent literature (e.g., Meyer and Allen, 1991; Meyer, Allen, and Smith, 1993) identified three dimensions of organizational commitment: affective commitment, continuance commitment, and normative commitment:

1. *Affective Commitment.* Affective commitment is an affective or emotional attachment to the organization, such that the strongly committed individual identifies with, is involved in,

and enjoys membership in the organization (Porter et al., 1974). Affective commitment is also defined as the degree to which an individual is psychologically attached to an employing organization through feelings such as loyalty, affection, warmth, belongingness, fondness, happiness, pleasure, and so on (Jaros, Jermier, Koehler, and Sincich, 1993).

2. *Continuance Commitment.* Continuance commitment is a tendency to engage in consistent lines of activity based on the individual recognition of the costs (or lost side bets) associated with discounting the activity (Becker, 1960). Continuance commitment is an instrumental view of organizational commitment. Leaving the organization can bear heavy costs for the employee who acts as an economic agent. These costs are weighted against the advantage of remaining, and when they are superior to the advantages, the employee is likely to stay within the organization. The expressed commitment will therefore not be due to any emotional attachment to the organization, but to the result of a sound calculation of the costs associated with leaving the organization or the benefits associated with staying in the organization. The costs may be the lack of better alternatives or the loss of material advantages, such as pension plans, opportunity of promotion, seniority, and so forth. The investments or side bets an employee makes in an organization, such as time, job effort, and the development of work friendships, organization-specific skills, and political deals, constitute sunk costs that diminish the attractiveness of external employment alternatives (Jaros, et al., 1993).

3. *Normative Commitment.* Normative commitment refers to the obligation to remain in the organization (Meyer and Allen, 1991; Meyer, Allen, and Smith, 1993). Normative commitment mostly calls for an obligation an employee must have toward his or her organization. Several studies (e.g., Folger and Konovsky, 1989; Sweeney and McFarlin, 1993) have attempted to study the impact of perceived fairness on organ-

izational commitment. "When a person's sense of fair treatment is seriously violated, that person's major response is to
reduce the sense of psychological belonging or commitment
to the group rather than to try to decrease the direct inputs or
increase the share of outcomes" (Organ and Konovsky, 1989,
427–428). As noticed by Lind and Tyler (1988), when group
procedures are fair, evaluation of the group and the commitment to the group will increase. Authorities' attitudes and behaviors shape subordinates' commitment to the group or
organization. "When deciding the extent to which they will
be loyal to a group or a relationship, people focus on the manner in which group decisions are made. If they believe that
such decisions are made fairly, then group members are more
inclined to accept a long-term commitment to the group."
(Lind and Tyler, 1988, 225–226)

McFarlin and Sweeney (1992) studied the effect of perceived fairness on organizational commitment. They found that procedural justice was a good predictor of organizational commitment. This result
confirms early findings (e.g., Folger and Konovsky, 1989) on the effects of justice perceptions on organizational commitment. However,
this effect was stronger for procedural justice than for distributive justice. The fairness of a firm's procedures may have a greater impact on
organizational commitment than the fairness of personal outcomes
(McFarlin and Sweeney, 1992). "Organizational commitment is enhanced among employees who believe that they are being treated as resources to be developed rather than as commodities to buy or sell"
(Zeffane, 1994, 1000).

These different studies, however, did not specify the types of organizational commitment affected by the different dimensions of fairness.
Beugré (1996) conducted a field study on the impact of fairness on different dimensions of organizational commitment. The author found
that procedural justice, which focuses on formal procedures, systemic
justice (perceptions of the organization as a fair system), and interactional justice (interpersonal relations) were positively related to affec-

tive commitment. The fairness of these types of justice may elicit positive affect in the employee who may be motivated to identify with the organization.

ORGANIZATIONAL CITIZENSHIP BEHAVIOR

"Organizational citizenship behavior (OCB) represents individual behavior that is discretionary, not directly or explicitly recognized by the formal system, and that, in the aggregate promotes the effective functioning of the organization" (Organ, 1988, 4). Smith, Organ, and Near (1983) and Organ (1988) distinguished two types of organizational citizenship behavior: one that benefits the organization in general (volunteering to serve in committees), and the other directed primarily at individuals within the organization (interpersonal helping). Several studies (e.g., Organ, 1988; Organ and Konovsky, 1989; Schnake, 1991) found a positive relationship between perceived fairness and organizational citizenship behavior. Organ (1990) found that the degree to which an employee feels fairly treated influences his or her tendency to engage in extra role behaviors. Employees who are fairly treated tend to increase their citizenship behavior compared to those who feel unfairly treated. Schnake (1991, 753) argues that "a general sense of fairness may lead employees to not worry whether a certain activity is required or whether they are going above and beyond the call of duty."

In studying the relationship between violation of psychological contract and organizational citizenship behavior, Robinson and Morrison (1995, 289) found that employees were less likely to display civic virtue behavior when they felt that their organization had failed to provide promised relational obligations such as career development and training: "A psychological contract is a set of beliefs regarding mutual obligations between employee and employer." The authors contend that "violation of a promise might be considered a form of unfair treatment, in the sense that the injustice is rooted in the act of betrayal rather than the outcome, per se. Thus, it might be a sense of betrayal or unfair treatment that leads to the erosion of trust, and hence, the erosion of organizationally-directed organizational citizenship behavior."

This result may also be interpreted in light of equity theory. "Employees attempt to maintain an equitable balance between their contributions and what they receive from their organization. When they believe their organization has failed to provide sufficient outputs, by not fulfilling promised obligations, they may withhold their discretionary inputs" (296).

Kim and Mauborgne (1996) conducted a field study on subsidiary top managers. They found that exercise of procedural justice inspired managers to go beyond the call of duty and engage in innovative actions, spontaneous cooperation, and creative behavior on behalf of the execution of decisions. They also found that procedural justice was related to commitment decisions, in-role behavior, and extra-role behavior. Kim and Mauborgne (1997, 66) note that "fair process profoundly influences attitudes and behaviors critical to high performance. It builds trust and unlocks ideas. With it, managers can achieve even the most painful and difficult goals while gaining the voluntary cooperation of the employees affected."

Farh, Podsakoff, and Organ (1990) studied the effects of leader behavior on subordinates' organizational citizenship behavior. They found that leader fairness increases subordinates' satisfaction and organizational citizenship behavior. Subordinates who felt that the leader was fair were likely to help their coworkers. This result was further supported by Deluga (1994, 323), who concluded that "fairness was the supervisor trust building behavior most closely associated with subordinate conscientiousness, sportsmanship, courtesy, and altruism."

Thus far, I have discussed the impact of fairness perceptions on employee attitudes and behaviors. But, what happens when employees feel unfairly treated? Do they leave the organization, or do they engage in disruptive behaviors such as theft and workplace aggression? I have analyzed three reactions: turnover, theft, and workplace aggression following a perceived injustice.

TURNOVER

A distinction should be made between turnover as an actual behavior, and turnover intentions (desire to leave one's organization). Turnover intention is an attitude, whereas actual turnover is a behavior. In a study of about 2,800 federal employees, Alexander and Ruderman (1987) found that justice perceptions influence turnover intentions. When employees felt unfairly treated, they expressed intentions to leave their jobs. However, turnover intentions were more related to distributive justice than to procedural justice. Lind and Tyler (1988) argue that workers who feel that evaluation procedures are unfair are more likely to leave their jobs. Dailey and Delaney (1992) contend that despite the quality of the work environment or how well employees like the work itself, when they believe that they are not respected and treated fairly by their managers, they will naturally turn their thoughts to quitting. However, when employees feel fairly treated, they may display positive behaviors such as organizational citizenship behavior. Mowday, Porter, and Steers (1982) also found that perceived unfairness tends to increase absenteeism and turnover.

Van Yperen, Hagedoorn, and Geurts (1996) conducted a field research in two manufacturing plants in the Netherlands. They found that employees who felt deprived were more apt to quit and to report sick than those who felt advantaged. This result supports previous findings (e.g., Alexander and Ruderman, 1987; Lind and Tyler, 1988) about the relationship between perceived unfairness and turnover. However, it is likely that turnover depends on other variables than perceptions of fairness alone. For instance, the availability of attractive alternatives may moderate the fairness-turnover relationship. Employees who feel unfairly treated may be likely to quit their organization when other alternatives are available. In a case of no better alternatives, they may decide to stay, despite apparent injustices. In such situations, they may tolerate the perceived injustices or engage in disruptive actions such as theft.

EMPLOYEE THEFT

Theft is defined as a nonviolent form of property deviance focused on one's company, committed by an employee of that company for personal gain (Greenberg and Scott, 1996). Employee theft includes activities such as the removal of products, supplies, materials, funds, data, information, or intellectual property (Greenberg, 1997). Why do employees engage in such behaviors? In other words, why do employees steal from their company? Research in organizational behavior (Greenberg, 1987b, 1990b, 1993b, 1997; Greenberg and Scott, 1996) suggests that employees steal from their company to react to inequities and unfair treatment. According to Greenberg and Scott, theft can be understood as an attempt to behaviorally redress a perceived inequitable state between parties. In this case, theft can be seen as a *restitution response*, a way of getting even with the organization because the employee did not receive a deserved outcome or a *retaliation response*, a way of punishing the organization for having harmed the employee. The authors state that in addition to stealing for purposes of evening the score between themselves and their employers, employees also steal to retaliate against institutions they believe have harmed them. An inequitable situation may encourage employees to steal, but poor treatment may fuel any perceived inequity and exacerbate the theft response.

People steal in response to feelings of underpayment (Greenberg, 1990a; Hollinger and Clark, 1983). Supporting this, Greenberg (1993a) found that underpaid employees tend to steal in order to compensate for their feeling of inequity; however, the author found that two factors—validity of information and interpersonal sensitivity shown to the underpaid victim—help reduce the tendency to steal. Greenberg (1993b) argues that uncaring and inconsiderate supervision are key determinants of employee theft. DeMore, Fisher, and Baron (1988) found that college students who felt unfairly treated used vandalism as a way of restoring justice. If employees steal to react to inequities and unfair treatment, they also engage in more destructive behaviors which go beyond pilferage. Workplace aggression is such a behavior which may stem from perceptions of injustice.

WORKPLACE AGGRESSION

Workplace aggression involves efforts by individuals to harm others with whom they work, or have worked, or the organizations in which they are presently, or were previously employed (Baron and Neuman,

1996; Neuman and Baron, 1997). This harmdoing is intentional, and includes psychological as well as physical injury. Workplace aggression is a broad concept, which includes workplace violence and takes several forms: name-calling, threats, refusal to obey company policies, destruction of company property, fist fights (Baron and Neuman, 1996).

Aggression can be covert or overt (Baron and Neuman,1996; Berkowitz, 1989; Buss, 1961). Covert aggression includes actions designed to harm others, but in ways that conceal the identity of the aggressor and/or the goal of such behavior. Such forms of aggression permit individuals to harm others, while minimizing the risk of retaliation or censure for such actions (Baron and Neuman, 1996). In real life, especially in organizations, several aggressors tend to use covert forms of aggression to avoid retaliation or punishments from the organization.

Baron and Neuman found that covert forms of aggression (verbal, indirect, passive) were more frequent in workplaces than overt forms of aggression (physical, direct, active). Specifically, employees rated verbal forms of aggression, especially forms that were also either indirect or passive in nature, as the most frequent forms they have both witnessed and experienced. These findings were further supported by Baron, Neuman, and Geddes (1997).

Baron, Neuman, and Geddes (1997) identified three forms of workplace aggression: expressions of hostility, obstructionism, and overt aggression. Expressions of hostility include behaviors which are verbal or symbolic in nature. Obstructionism includes behaviors that are passive in nature and tend to obstruct or impede the target's performance. Finally, overt aggression includes behaviors that may be considered workplace violence, such as physical assaults or destruction of company property. Although different, these three dimensions of workplace aggression may be related. Before acting or reacting overtly, a person may attempt to obstruct another or express hostility toward him or her. Such actions, especially obstructionism, are hard to identify and thereby sanction. The potential aggressor may use overt action if the threat of retaliation is minimum.

Research on aggression by Berkowitz (1989) suggests that people are likely to become aggressive if they believe that someone has un-

fairly tried to hurt them. The author also argues that illegitimately im-
posed barriers to goal attainment are more likely to produce aggressive
responses than those that seem to be socially proper, but even the latter
can activate an instigation to aggression. Employees seek various goals
in their professional lives; any actions which prevent them from reaching their goals may be perceived as hostile and lay the ground for subsequent negative reactions, including aggression. According to
Berkowitz, a barrier keeping people from reaching an attractive goal
they had expected to obtain can lead to open aggression.

Folger and Baron (1996), O'Leary-Kelly, Griffin, and Glew
(1996), and Greenberg and Alge (in press) have hypothesized that perceptions of justice may influence workplace aggression. O'Leary-
Kelly, Griffin, and Glew (1996, 235) suggest that "employers who ensure fair treatment will have more satisfied and less aggressive employees." Beugré (1996) found that perceptions of justice did, in fact,
influence workplace aggression. The author found that systemic justice negatively predicted workplace aggression. When employees felt
that the organization was a fair system, they tended to report less aggression. Baron, Neuman, and Geddes (1997) found that perceptions
of fairness influenced the three identified types of workplace aggression. However, respondents tended to express more obstructionist behaviors and hostility than overt aggression.

If employees react to justice by displaying pro-organizational
behaviors, and injustices by displaying antisocial behaviors, then it is
important to develop strategies to enhance perceptions of fairness
while reducing perceptions of unfairness.

7

Applying Justice Concepts in Organizations

This chapter develops a practical orientation of organizational justice, focusing on how managers can create fair working environments and at the same time avoid the pitfalls of acting unjustly. It contains three main sections: first, an integrative model of organizational justice; second, an instrument for measuring perceptions of justice in organizations (see Beugré and Baron, 1997), and finally, suggested ways of creating fair working environments.

AN INTEGRATIVE MODEL OF ORGANIZATIONAL JUSTICE

The integrative model of organizational justice (e.g., Figure 1) contends that perceptions of justice are shaped by two sets of variables: individual and organizational. Demographic characteristics (gender, level of education, occupational status, and tenure within the organization), personality variables (negative affectivity, hostile attribution bias), and cognitive attributes (self-serving bias, causal attributions) are considered individual variables influencing perceptions of fairness. Organizational variables include organizational change, performance appraisal, leader behavior, pay, punishment, selection, and organizational culture. The effects of these antecedent variables on perceptions of justice have been discussed in-depth in chapters 4 and 5. For in-

Figure 1
An Integrative Model of the Antecedents and Consequences of Organizational Justice

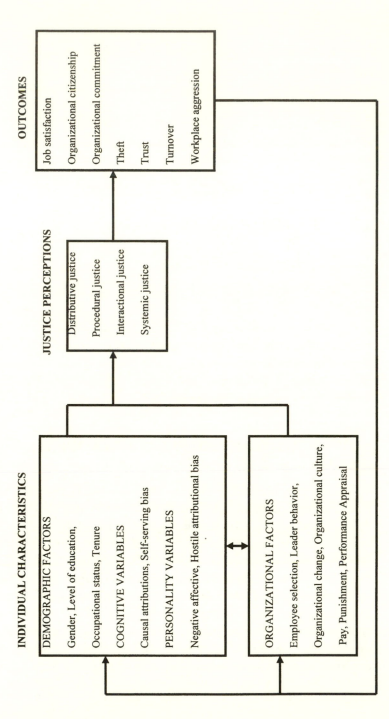

stance, negative affectivity, a personality variable, may influence perceptions of fairness. Similarly, a supervisor's behavior may influence perceptions of fairness. Although these antecedents taken separately may affect perceptions of justice, they may also interact to influence individuals' justice judgments. A high negative affectivity individual would tend to perceive a given punishment as unfair, compared to a low negative affectivity individual. Similarly, an employee would feel unjustly treated when he or she attributes his or her supervisor's behavior to hostile intentions.

Perceptions of fairness elicit attitudinal (job satisfaction, commitment, trust) and behavioral (organizational citizenship behavior, turnover, workplace aggression) reactions. Other reactions, such as cooperation, helping behavior, and performance, may also be induced by perceptions of fairness, although research on the effects of justice on such behavioral outcomes is scant. Perceptions of fair treatment may lead to positive attitudes and behaviors, whereas perceptions of unfair treatment may induce dysfunctional attitudes and behaviors. Although the list of attitudes and behaviors included in the model is not exhaustive, it represents the types of attitudes and behaviors described in the literature on organizational justice.

The integrative model of organizational justice has both theoretical and practical implications. On the theoretical stand, it may help organizational justice scholars to rely on a theoretical framework describing the antecedents and consequences of justice perceptions in organizations. On the practical side, the model would help managers to understand the determinants and consequences of perceptions of justice in the workplace. First, they should understand what variables are likely to induce a feeling of fairness. A manager's behavior may be interpreted in several ways by his or her subordinates, depending on their social background, the values they believe in, their expectations of a proper behavior from a manager, their own personality, and so on. Second, managers may develop appropriate strategies when they clearly understand the antecedents and consequences of justice perceptions. Such understanding may contribute to the developing of appropriate training programs. Training that has a theoretical foundation is likely to be effective because theory allows understanding on the part of organizational decision makers.

MEASURING ORGANIZATIONAL JUSTICE

Managers cannot learn to create fair working environments unless they understand organizational justice components and are able to measure them. In this section, I present an organizational justice scale (see Beugré, 1996 and Beugré and Baron, 1997 for more details on the psychometric properties of the scale). The organizational justice scale (OJS) was developed to measure four dimensions of organizational justice: distributive, procedural, interactional, and systemic (Beugré and Baron, 1997). Empirical research for the scale was realized in a pilot study of sixty-one participants, and then in a main study including a larger sample (232 employees). The original scale contained seventy-five items. After the pilot study, the number of items was reduced to forty-one. Results of the main study on 232 employees were factor analyzed and yielded four factors, representing respectively, distributive justice (ten items), procedural justice (five items), interactional justice (ten items) and systemic justice (ten items). The scale is presented in Exhibit 1.

The importance of building an instrument to measure organizational justice was underscored by Greenberg (1990a). Previous instruments were ad hoc, developed for specific studies. Because of their ad hoc nature, it was practically impossible for managers as well as organizational scholars to rely on them for further investigations. Furthermore, it was impossible for managers to use them as instruments to assess perceptions of fair treatment in their organizations. It is my expectation that with the OJS, managers will finally measure how fairly their employees feel treated. Results of the OJS may help develop ways of improving fairness in an organization.

CREATING FAIR WORKING ENVIRONMENTS

If justice matters in today's workplace, it is important for managers to create fair working environments. Such efforts would be beneficial,

Exhibit 1
Items of the Organizational Justice Scale

Distributive Justice

1. Overall the rewards I receive here are quite fair.
2. My most recent raise gave me the full amount I deserve.
3. My pay is appropriate given my performance.
4. My pay is appropriate given my responsibilities.
5. I am fairly rewarded taking into account the amount of education I have had.
6. I am fairly rewarded considering the amount of training I have had.
7. I am fairly rewarded in view of the experience I have.
8. I am fairly rewarded for the amount of effort I put forth.
9. I am fairly rewarded for work I have done well.
10. I am fairly rewarded considering the level of stress in my job.

Procedural Justice

11. Objective procedures are used in evaluating my performance.
12. My input is considered in evaluating my performance.
13. My supervisor gets input from me before a recommendation.
14. My performance evaluation is based on accurate information.
15. My input on what I could do to improve company performance is solicited.

Interactional Justice

16. When decisions are made about my job, my supervisor treats me with kindness and consideration.
17. I am treated with respect and dignity in this company.
18. When decisions are made bout my job, my supervisor is sensitive to my personal needs.
19. When decisions are made about my job, my supervisor shows concern for my rights as an employee.
20. Concerning decisions made about my job, my supervisor discusses their implications with me.
21. My supervisor offers adequate justification for decisions made about my job.
22. When making decisions about my job, my supervisor offers explanations that make sense to me.
23. My supervisor explains very clearly any decisions made about my job.
24. I have friendly relations with my supervisor.
25. My supervisor is completely candid and frank with me.

Systemic Justice

26. Overall, all decisions in this company are fair.
27. Fairness is an important objective in this company.
28. In this company, job decisions are made in an unbiased manner.

Cont'd

29. In this company, all employee concerns are heard before job decisions are made.

30. In this company, job decisions are based on accurate information.

31. In this company, job decisions are based on complete information.

32. In this company, additional information about job decisions is provided when requested by employees.

33. In this company, all decisions are applied consistently across all affected employees.

34. The culture of this company encourages fairness.

35. In this company, disciplinary actions are always fairly implemented.

not only for their organizations, but mostly for their own careers. For this purpose, managers should integrate justice concerns at four levels: distributive, procedural, interactional, and systemic justice. Following is an analysis of how managers should enhance perceptions of justice at these four levels.

Enhancing Distributive Justice

As we have seen, distributive justice plays an important role in people's lives. How different outcomes are distributed raises concerns for justice judgments. However, one must recognize that organizational resources are scarce and cannot be allocated to everyone at the same type and according to the amount desired. Managers are often required to make difficult decisions in allocating rewards and punishments. Such decisions often raise concerns for distributive justice. There are several ways of ensuring distributive justice in organizations.

One way to increase perceptions of distributive fairness is to tie rewards to performance. In so doing, each employee should be informed about how the pay, raise, or promotion is given, as well as how the level of a salary corresponds to his or her accomplishments. Such an effort may include the participation of the employee in setting the level of his or her compensation. Managers should be trained to understand the consequences of their actions in terms of fairness. For instance, employees should see a clear link between their contributions and the rewards they get, in terms of compensation, promotion, or demotion. A compensation which ties outcomes to performance may certainly contribute to perceptions of distributive fairness.

Punishment and other negative outcomes such as demotion, should correspond to the gravity of the behavior incriminated. The punishment should fit the crime, and be timely, not delayed. A punishment which occurs long after the deed has been committed may be perceived as unfair. Managers should be aware that their decisions may influence other employees who witness a punishment. The extent to which observers perceive managers' decisions as fair (or unfair) may influence their subsequent reactions.

In chapter 5, I have argued that organizational changes, pay, and performance appraisal influence perceptions of justice. Distributive justice is particularly important when allocating rewards such as pay and bonuses. To the extent that these rewards are proportional to the employee's inputs, he or she will perceive them as fair. However, any discrepancy between what the employee perceives as a fair outcome and the actual outcome may raise feelings of distributive injustice. Managers can therefore enhance distributive justice by allocating rewards that are proportional to inputs. Distributive justice is also important in situations of dramatic changes (Cobb, Wooten, and Folger, 1995; Beugré, 1997; Novelli, Kirkman, and Shapiro (1995). Change most often involves layoffs, demotions, and the like. Positive as well as negative outcomes during a change process should be fairly allocated. In addition to distributive justice, managers should also consider the fairness of formal methods and procedures.

Enhancing Procedural Justice

Managers may enhance procedural justice by developing mechanisms that favor employee empowerment and give them voice. "One clear indicant of procedural justice for an organization is to have some mechanisms in place that will see to it that workers do have a say about things that happen at work" (McFarlin and Sweeney, 1996, 300). Magner, Rahman, and Walker (1996) suggest that managers should avoid using capricious and arbitrary procedures in allocating constrained work resources. For this purpose, managers should develop clear company rules and policies and voice mechanisms.

Clear Company Rules and Policies

Companies should have clear, written rules and policies which are communicated to employees, as well as grievance procedures available to employees. The existence of such procedures would positively influence perceptions of procedural fairness. For instance, managers should be trained to understand the different rules and procedures so that they may be able to communicate them to employees when and where needed. The availability of clear rules signifies to employees that managers cannot abuse their power. These rules and policies should be communicated to employees through discussions or be available in form of documentation. Leventhal, Karuza, and Fry's (1980) six rules of: consistency, bias suppression, accuracy, correctability, representativeness, and ethicality can be used to enhance perceptions of fair treatment. To the extent that managerial decisions follow these rules, they may be perceived as fair.

Voice Mechanisms

Folger (1977) has shown that voice leads to perceptions of fairness. When employees are involved in the decisions concerning their jobs or the outcomes they perceive, they are likely to consider these decisions fair. Providing voice mechanisms ensure employees that the organization is ready to accept their complaints. However, the opportunity to voice one's opinions alone does not provide perceptions of fair treatment.

Enhancing Interactional Justice

Interactional justice can be enhanced by providing outcome information in a considerate, socially sensitive manner (Bies and Shapiro, 1988; Brockner and Greenberg, 1990; Greenberg, 1994). Respect for employees tends to induce feelings of fair treatment and thereby enhance employee commitment and trust in the organization and its managers.

Provide Causal Accounts

Providing explanations for decisions enhances the perceived fairness of these decisions (Bies, 1987; Bies and Shapiro, 1988; Greenberg, 1994). To enhance perceptions of interactional justice, managers should treat employees with respect and dignity and give detailed explanations for their actions. A decision which cannot stand scrutiny is perceived as unfair. The provision of causal accounts may create a climate of fairness and trustworthy relationship between a manager and his or her subordinates.

Deliver Timely Feedback

Give timely feedback to employees regarding their performance. Feedback allows employees to know how well (or bad) they are doing in their job. Such feedback helps to adjust employees' work behaviors. But not all feedback is "good news" for employees; negative feedback should be delivered to employees in a respectful manner. Baron (1993) suggests that negative feedback leads to perceptions of unfairness and is negatively perceived by those who receive it.

Enhancing Systemic Justice

Perceptions of distributive, procedural, and interactional justice will lead to perceptions of the organization as a fair system. For instance, a customer who is fairly treated by a company's sales representative will consider this experience as positive, and thereby will make an impression about the company as a whole. Beugré and Baron (1997) found that distributive justice predicted systemic justice. When employees felt that outcome distribution was fair, they tended to consider that a fair system had engendered it. The same result was found when the authors analyzed the effect of procedural justice and interactional justice on systemic justice. They also found that perceptions of procedural fairness and interactional fairness positively influenced perceptions of systemic justice. Managers may also enhance perceptions of systemic justice by developing strong organizational cultures and a general climate of fairness.

To the extent that managers behave fairly, they are likely to create a general impression of the organization as a fair system. As stated by Greenberg (1996, 100), "Just as an individual may seek a reputation as fair-minded, so too might an entire organization strive for an image as a place that treats its employees and customers fairly." Behaving fairly is beneficial for the organization, in that it may help attract and keep talented employees and gain customers' loyalty. Greenberg (1990c) notes that an organization with an established culture of fairness might reap the benefits of attracting and maintaining the best candidates and capturing the business of customers who are impressed by that corporate image. Organizational justice may be enhanced through appropriate training.

ENHANCING ORGANIZATIONAL JUSTICE THROUGH TRAINING

Managers can be trained on how to behave fairly in their organizations. Although such efforts are scant in the literature on organizational justice, the few studies that have tested the effects of training on managers' ability to behave fairly have yielded promising results. Skarlicki and Latham (1996) found that training in organizational justice can help enhance organizational citizenship behavior (OCB). After the authors trained participants for three months, they found that perceptions of union fairness among members whose leaders were in the training group were significantly higher than among members whose leaders were in the control group. The authors identified two dimensions of citizenship behaviors: behavior supporting the union as an organization, and behavior supporting union members. Citizenship behavior on both dimensions was significantly higher among union members whose leaders were trained. An organizational justice training program should include the factors influencing perceptions of fairness, as well as the consequences of fairness.

Cole and Latham (1997) conducted a study aimed to train supervisors in procedural justice. Participants were trained using a combination of lectures, group discussions, and role-plays over five day-held sessions. The experimental group comprised thirty-five supervisors, and the control group, thirty-six supervisors. Participants in the experimental group were trained to take effective disciplinary actions with subordinates, whereas those of the control group did not receive such training. Cole and Latham found that unionized employees and disciplinary subject matters (managers, union officials, and attorneys) rated the trained supervisors higher on disciplinary fairness behavior than the supervisors in the control group. The trained supervisors also had higher self-efficacy related to employee discipline than did untrained supervisors.

The results of these two studies showed that fairness in organizations can be improved through training. Managers should be trained in how to deliver bad news as well as good news. Also important is the provision of causal accounts. To the extent that employees receive detailed information about decisions concerning their jobs, they are likely to express feelings of fair treatment. As stated by Greenberg (1996, 98), "participatory decision-making in organizations may be believed to be fairer than more autocratic procedures." Since justice in the workplace is of substantial importance to workers, organized labor, and management (Fryxell and Gordon, 1989), organizations should develop training programs aimed to enhance fairness.

Conclusion

Throughout this book, I have discussed the importance of fairness in organizations. This analysis, although not exhaustive, shows that considerations of fairness are important in organizational behavior. I have deliberately focused on justice within organizations, not only discussing the causes and reactions to perceptions of justice, but also suggesting ways of creating fair working environments. Although this book represents an important contribution to the literature in organizational justice, I am aware of its limitations. For instance, not only should companies behave fairly with their employees (micro-organizational fairness), but they should also act fairly with their outside stakeholders (macro-organizational fairness). Justice matters in areas such as strategic alliances, customer satisfaction, and environmental protection. In an era of economic globalization, cross-cultural issues in justice perceptions are also important. Although some of these issues have been addressed by organizational justice scholars, more research is needed to better understand the role of justice perceptions in these areas.

FAIRNESS ISSUES IN ACQUISITIONS AND MERGERS

Acquisitions occur when one organization takes over another (Citera and Rentsch, 1993). Acquired organizations are often smaller than acquiring organizations, while mergers frequently occur between organizations of similar sizes (Rentsch and Schneider, 1991). A merger is a combination of two organizations of relatively equal size (Walsh, 1988). Why is it important to discuss issues of fairness in acquisitions and mergers? In such operations, fairness issues arise at two levels: the procedures used to negotiate the deal, the changes and their implementation. For instance, Citera and Rentsch (1993) note that the acquisition process consists of two stages: planning and implementation. During the first stage, discussions about the deal between managements of the two companies are held. At this stage, such factors as degree of friendliness or hostility may shape future relations. Decisions made during the negotiation process may be seen by both parties as fair or unfair. In the case of mergers, since the two organizations are often of the same size, it is possible that an equilibrium be obtained between them. Both organizations may have equal responsibility in making important decisions concerning the merger.

The situation is quite different when we consider acquisition in which a more "powerful" organization acquires a smaller one. In this situation, managers of the acquiring organization tend to have their views prevail in initiating and implementing the changes. Managers and employees of the acquired organization may experience frustration and feel resentment toward their counterparts of the acquiring organization. This resentment may lead to low commitment from employees and decrease productivity. Some managers and employees of the acquired organization may decide to leave. In a longitudinal study, Walsh (1988) found that top management turnover rates following a merger or acquisition were significantly higher than "normal" top management turnover rates. Although the author did not provide an explanation about the causes of these high rates of turnover, one may suspect that stress, uncertainty, and perceived unfairness following the acquisition or merger explain it in part. Some authors (e.g., Citera and Rentsch, 1993) contend that open communication may help reduce the negative feelings and uncertainty related to dysfunctional outcomes, as well as help employees to understand the reasons of the acquisition or the merger and the necessity of changes. This open communication may also reduce potential resistance to the strategic alliance.

FAIRNESS AND CUSTOMER SATISFACTION

Although external to the organization itself, the customer is part of its feedback loop (Clemmer, 1993). Therefore, fairness considerations may apply to the relationship between the organization and its customers. According to Clemmer, fairness concerns may occur at least at three levels:

1. Is what the customer gets at a reasonable price? In other words, is the ratio quality/price fair? Answers to these questions refer to fairness of the outcome.

2. The manner in which the organization deals with the customer refers to procedural justice. For instance, was a delay in delivering a product or service reasonable? Is there a claim procedure when the customer is unsatisfied with a service or product?

3. Is there an informational relationship between the customer and the company? How is the relation perceived by the customer? This refers to interactional justice.

In discussing fairness issues in services, Gronroos (1984) notes that delivering a service implies both a process and an outcome. The process refers to the manner in which the service is delivered, while the outcome refers to the service itself. The author refers to technical quality as the object of the service, and functional quality as the interactions with the customer. In a competitive economy, companies must capitalize on interactions with customers to gain their loyalty. Issues of fairness are also important in decisions related to the protection of the natural environment.

FAIRNESS AND ENVIRONMENTAL ISSUES

Pressures from environmentalists (e.g., social groups advocating environmental issues) have led companies to become aware of the consequences of their operations on the natural environment. According to Opotow and Clayton (1994), justice aspects of environmental issues are important in determining how people relate to the environment and in motivating people to take an environmental stance. Environmental justice is relevant in the allocation of natural resources and man-made hazards both between and within countries. The authors contend that both procedural justice, with its focus on the fairness of decision-making processes, and distributive justice, with its focus on norms for resource distribution, are important aspects of these environmental conflicts.

Environmental justice refers to the need to distribute environmental hazards fairly across different demographic groups, and to connect environmental concerns with issues of social justice (Opotow and Clayton, 1994). According to environmental justice scholars (e.g., Stern and Dietz, 1994), three types of beliefs influence individuals' attitudes toward the environment: egoistic values, altruistic values, and biospheric values. Egoistic values predispose people to protect aspects of the environment that affect them personally or to oppose protection of the environment if the personal costs are high; altruistic values predispose an individual to protect aspects of the environment if the consequences benefit others or the costs are too high for them and the society. Finally, biospheric values predispose people to judge phenomena on the basis of their costs or benefits to ecosystems or the biosphere. In analyzing the impact of values on individuals' attitudes toward the environment, Axelrod (1994) found that people with universal value orientation were consistently more prone to endorse environmentally protective actions than were their economically oriented counterparts.

Most investigations on organizational justice have concerned the North American context. In today's global economy, it is important for managers and organizational scholars alike to understand the role of cultural issues on perceptions of justice. Meindl, Cheng, and Jun (1990, 198) suggest that "as globalization and modernization cut everywhere deeper into existing social fabrics and give rise to new social patterns, new hopes, new aspirations, new institutions, and new authority structures, basic conceptions of social and industrial justice naturally come under review, are challenged, and eventually are changed to define a new order."

JUSTICE ISSUES IN A GLOBAL ECONOMY

Granovetter (1985) contends that economic activities are embedded in a web of social relationships. "The particular cognitive and behavioral manifestations of justice, as they take place in the resolution of allocation problems, may be conditioned by the culture at large in which organizations are embedded" (Meindl, Cheng, and Jun, 1990, 224). This implies that since organizations are influenced by their social, cultural, and political environment, research on organizational justice should consider the impact of the external environment on employee perceptions of fair treatment. Some authors (Gundykunst and Ting-Tomey, 1988; James, 1993; Meindl, Cheng, and Jun, 1990), however, have noticed the cultural relativity of justice evaluations. Every social system has procedures that regulate the distribution of rewards and resources. "The procedures and distributions they generate are properties of the social system, but are also reflected in individual behavior and beliefs" (Leventhal, Karuza, and Fry, 1980, 169).

Hofstede (1980) identified four dimensions of culture: power distance, individualism/collectivism, uncertainty avoidance, and feminism/masculinism. James (1993) contends that power distance influences perceptions of fairness, and tolerance to unfairness, and in societies, higher in power distance, people tend to tolerate injustice. Cultures that inculcate an acceptance of power differences lead individuals to expect, take for granted and, therefore, not get angry about injustices. Conversely, in relatively low-power distance cultures, there is less a tendency to defer to power, which inclines individuals to react negatively when situations or other individuals seem to be treating them unfairly (Gundykunst and Ting-Tomey, 1988). Cultures favoring unconditional deference and allegiance to authority may lead people to accept unfair practices and capricious decisions from authorities.

Culture may also influence allocation rules. Murphy-Berman, Berman, Sigh, Pachauri, and Kumar (1984) found that people from the United States were much more inclined toward an equity principle and less toward a need principle than people from India when allocating positive outcomes. However, when the outcomes were negative, such as cuts in pay, both subjects gave preference to those with the greatest needs. According to the authors, this tendency may depend on human nature, suggesting that one has to be compassionate with those who are deprived and less fortunate. In comparing results relative to perceived fairness and allocation norms between Chinese and American managers, Meindl, Cheng, and Jun (1990) found that the definition of fairness and the preferences for highly differentiated, equity-based allocation schemes among the Chinese managers were similar to those of their American counterparts. However, unlike American managers, Chinese managers were inflexible in their ratings. The authors considered the inflexibility of the Chinese managers as "symptomatic of an internal struggle with the necessity of becoming committed to forward-looking reforms and an attendant psychological reactance with the preferences and values associated with prereform ideologies of the past" (233).

In another comparative study between American and Korean students, Leung and Park (1986) found that Korean students showed a stronger relation between the allocation rule a person uses and his or her friendliness than did American students. An allocator using equity rule was perceived as less friendly than one who used an equality rule. In a field study, Sugawara and Huo (1994) found that Japanese employees were more concerned with procedural justice issues, although distributive justice was not neglected. They note that clarity and openness of procedures are related to procedural justice.

Itoi, Obhuci, and Fukuno (1996) found that Japanese respondents showed more preferences for mitigating accounts such as apologies and excuses, whereas American respondents showed more preferences for assertive accounts such as justifications. These findings suggest that Japanese participants' mitigating style reflects a stronger concern for relationship and social harmony, whereas American participants' assertive style reveals a stronger concern for personal satisfaction. More frequently than the Americans, the Japanese used denial or gave no account in conflicts with strangers, although they showed a general tendency to use apologies in conflict situations. This result indicates that in collectivist cultures, people are likely to enter in conflict with out-group members. However, in the same research, the authors found that when the "harm was severe, both Japanese and American participants more frequently abandoned the assertive accounts in favor of mitigating tactics" (928).

Meindl, Cheng, and Jun (1990) compared justice perceptions in collectivist and individual societies. A collectivist culture impacts to its members value systems in which a consideration of whole social groups or units is placed ahead of the partisan interests of subgroups and individual actors. "Individualistic cultures generate orientations in members whereby the fulfillment of individual interests supersede any conception of group interests" (225). The authors found that collectivist cultures tended to favor equality rules, whereas individualistic cultures tended to favor equity rules. Leung and Lind (1986) conducted a cross-national comparison of legal systems in the United States and Hong Kong. College students of both cultures were asked to indicate their preferences for using adversary and nonadversary procedures. Two additional factors were the status of the investigator in the dispute resolution procedure, and the gender of the participant. Results showed that American participants preferred the adversary procedure, whereas their Hong Kong counterparts were indifferent to both procedures. Investigator's status and gender interacted in their effects on American participants' preferences, but did not affect Hong Kong participants preferences. In both cultures, participants viewed the adversarial procedure as vesting more process in the hands of disputants.

In another comparative study, Steiner and Gilliland (1996) analyzed French and American students' attitudes toward selection techniques in both countries. College students from both countries rated the favorability of ten selection procedures and indicated their reactions on seven procedural dimensions. Results showed that selection decisions based on interviews, work-sample tests and resumes were perceived favorably in both cultures. Graphology (often considered nonscientific) was perceived more favorably in France than in the United States. The authors also found that even in France, graphology was negatively perceived compared to other selection techniques. It appeared that participants in both cultures tended to view "objective" procedures as fairer than subjective ones. A familiarity effect tended to appear in their results. Participants tended to rank familiar procedures as fairer than nonfamiliar ones. For instance, graphology is a familiar selection technique to French participants, compared to their American counterparts. However, Marin (1981) did not find a difference related to cultures. The author compared American and Colombian samples, and found that equitable allocation was perceived as fairer by both groups. Both groups also preferred equitable allocation over equal allocation with a marked difference among Colombian participants. Lind, Tyler and Huo (1997) suggest that procedural justice is defined much the same way across different cultural contexts.

The different areas discussed are important avenues for further research in organizations. Individual behavior in organizations cannot be clearly understood if one ignores the external environments in which they operate. Similarly, several stakeholders including employees, managers, shareholders, customers, and policymakers are directly or indirectly influenced by an organization's activities. Integrating their concerns may help develop better management strategies.

References

Adams, S. J. (1963). Toward an understanding of inequity. *Journal of Abnormal Social Psychology, 67,* 422–436.

Adams, S. J. (1965). Inequity in social exchange. In L. Berkowitz (Ed.), *Advances in experimental social psychology* (Vol. 2, pp. 267–299). New York: Academic Press.

Adams, S. J., & Freedman, S. (1976). Equity theory revisited. Comments and annotated bibliography. In L. Berkowitz (Ed.), *Advances in experimental social psychology* (Vol. 9, pp. 43–90). New York: Academic Press.

Alexander, S., & Ruderman, M. (1987). The role of procedural and distributive justice in organizational behavior. *Social Justice Research, 1,* 177–198.

Allen, N. J., & Meyer, J. P. (1990). The measurement and antecedents of affective, continuance, and normative commitment to the organization. *Journal of Occupational Psychology, 63,* 1–18.

Aquino, K., Griffeth, R. W., Allen, D. G., & Hom, P. W. (1997). Integrating justice constructs into the turnover process: A test of a referent cognitions model. *The Academy of Management Journal, 40,* 1208–1227.

Arvey, R. D., & Jones, A. P. (1985). The use of discipline in organizational settings: A framework for future research. In L. L. Cummings & B. M. Staw (Eds.), *Research in organizational behavior* (Vol. 7, pp. 367–408). Greenwich, CT: JAI Press.

Asforth, B. E. (1992). The perceived inequity of systems. *Administration and Society, 24,* 375–408.

Averill, J. (1979). Anger. In H. Howe & R. Dienstbier (Eds.), *Nebraska symposium on motivation* (Vol. 26, pp. 1–80). Lincoln: University of Nebraska Press.

Axelrod, L. J. (1994). Balancing personal needs with environmental preservation: Identifying the values that guide decisions in ecological dilemmas. *Journal of Social Issues, 50,* 85–104.

Ball, A. G., Trevino, L. K., & Sims, P. H., Jr. (1993). Justice and organizational punishment: Attitudinal outcomes of disciplinary events. *Social Justice Research, 6,* 39–67.

Ball, A. G., Trevino, L. K., & Sims, P. H., Jr. (1994). Just and unjust punishment: Influences on subordinate performance and citizenship. *Academy of Management Journal, 37,* 299–322.

Bandura, A. (1977). Self-efficacy: Towards a unifying theory of behavioral change. *Psychological Review, 84,* 191–215.

Bandura, A. (1986). *Social foundations of thought and action: A social-cognitive view.* Englewood Cliffs, NJ: Prentice-Hall.

Baron, R. A. (1990). Environmentally-induced positive effect: Its impact on self-efficacy, task performance, negotiation, and conflict. *Journal of Applied Social Psychology, 20,* 368–384.

Baron, R. A. (1993). Criticism (informal negative feedback) as a source of perceived unfairness in organizations: Effects, mechanisms, and countermeasures. In R. Cropanzano (Ed.), *Justice in the workplace: Approaching fairness in human resource management* (pp. 155–170). Hillsdale, NJ: Lawrence Erlbaum Associates.

Baron, R. A., & Neuman, J. H. (1996). Workplace violence and workplace aggression: Evidence on their relative frequency and causes. *Aggressive Behavior, 22,* 161–173.

Baron, R. A., Neuman, J. H., & Geddes, D. (1997). *On the nature and consequences of workplace aggression: Hypotheses from basic research on human aggression.* Manuscript under review.

Baron, R. A., & Richardson, D. R. (1994). *Human aggression.* (2nd Ed). New York: Plenum Press.

Bazerman, M. H. (1993). Fairness, social comparison, and irrationality. In J. K. Murnighan (Ed.), *Social psychology in organizations: Advances in theory and research* (pp. 184–203). Englewood Cliffs, NJ: Prentice-Hall.

Becker, H. S. (1960). Notes on the concept of commitment. *American Journal of Sociology, 66*, 32–40.

Berg, N. E., & Mussen, P. (1975). The origins and development of concepts of justice. *Journal of Social Sciences, 31*, 183–201.

Berger, J., Zelditch, M., Anderson, B., & Cohen, B. P. (1972). Structural aspects of distributive justice: A status-value formulation. In J. Berger, M. Zelditch, & B. Anderson (Eds.), *Sociological theories in progress* (pp. 21–45). Boston: Houghton Mifflin.

Berkowitz, L. (1989). Frustration-aggression hypothesis: Examination and reformulation. *Psychological Bulletin, 106*, 59–73.

Beugré, C. D. (1996). *Analyzing the effects of perceived fairness on organizational commitment and workplace aggression.* Doctoral Dissertation. Rensselaer Polytechnic Institute. [printed 1997] Ann Arbor: UMI.

Beugré, C. D. (1997). *Effects of organizational change on perceived fairness and trust.* Manuscript submitted for publication.

Beugré, C. D., & Baron, R. A. (1997). *Understanding justice components and measuring the relationship between them.* Manuscript submitted for publication.

Bies, R. J. (1987). The predicament of injustice: The management of moral outrage. In L. L. Cummings, & B. W. Staw (Eds.), *Research in organizational behavior* (Vol. 9, pp. 289–319). Greenwich, CT: JAI Press.

Bies, R. J., & Moag, J. S. (1986). Interactional justice: Communication criteria of fairness. In R. Lewicki, B. H. Sheppard, & M. H. Bazerman (Eds.), *Research on negotiation in organizations* (Vol. 1, pp. 43–55). Greenwich, CT: JAI Press.

Bies, R. J., & Shapiro, D. L. (1987). Interactional fairness judgments: The influence of causal accounts. *Social Justice Research, 1*, 199–218.

Bies, R. J., & Shapiro, D. L. (1988). Voice and justification: Their influence on procedural fairness judgments. *Academy of Management Journal, 31*, 676–685.

Bies, R. J., Shapiro, D. L., & Cummings, L. L. (1988). Causal accounts and managing organizational conflict: It is not enough to say it's not my fault. *Communication Research, 15*, 381–399.

Bies, R. J., & Tripp, M. T. (1995). The use and abuse of power: Justice as social control. In R. Cropanzano & K. M. Kamar (Eds.), *Organizational politics, justice, and support* (pp. 131–145). Westport, CT: Quorum Books.

Blau, P. M. (1964). *Exchange and power in social life*. New York: Wiley.

Bobocel, R. D. (1996). Sex-based promotion decisions and interactional fairness: Investigating the influence of managerial accounts. *Journal of Applied Psychology, 81*, 22–35.

Boudreaux, J. W., & Rynes, S. L. (1985). The role of recruitment in staff utility analysis. *Journal of Applied Psychology, 70*, 354–366.

Boulding, K. E. (1956). General systems theory: The skeleton of science. *Management Science* (April), 197–208.

Bradley, G. W. (1978). Self-serving biases in the attribution process: A reexamination of the fact or fiction question. *Journal of Personality and Social Psychology, 36*, 56–71.

Brett, J. M. (1986). Commentary on procedural justice papers. In R. J. Lewicki, B. H. Sheppard, & M. H. Bazerman (Eds.), *Research on negotiation in organizations* (Vol. 1, pp. 81–90). Greenwich, CT: JAI Press.

Brockner, J. (1994). Perceived fairness and survivors' reactions to layoffs, or how downsizing organizations can do well by doing good. *Social Justice Research, 7*, 345–363.

Brockner, J., DeWitt, R. L., Grover, S., & Reed, T. (1987). When it is especially important to explain why: Factors affecting the relationship between managers' explanations of a layoff and survivors' reactions to the layoff. *Journal of Experimental Social Psychology, 26*, 389–407.

Brockner, J., & Greenberg, J. (1990). The impact of layoffs on survivors: An organizational justice perspective. In J. S. Carroll (Ed.), *Applied social psychology and organizational settings* (pp. 45–75). Hillsdale, NJ: Erlbaum Associates Publishers.

Brockner, J., Konovsky, M., Cooper-Schneider, R., Folger, R., Martin, C., & Bies, R. J. (1994). Interactive effects of procedural justice and outcome negativity on victims and survivors of job loss. *Academy of Management Journal, 37*, 397–409.

Brockner, J., & Siegel, P. (1995). Understanding the interaction between procedural and distributive justice. In R. M. Kramer & T. R. Tyler (Eds.), *Trust in organizations: Frontiers of theory and research* (pp. 390–423). Thousand Oaks, CA: Sage Publications.

Brockner, J., Tyler, R. T., & Cooper-Schneider, R. (1992). The influence of prior commitment to an institution on reactions to perceived unfairness: The higher they are, the harder they fall. *Administrative Science Quarterly, 37*, 241–261.

Brockner, J., & Wiesenfeld, B. M. (1996). An integrative framework for explaining reactions to decisions: Interactive effects of outcomes and procedures. *Psychological Bulletin, 120*, 189–208.

Bromiley, P., & Cummings, L. L. (1995). Organizations with trust: Theory and measurement. In R. Bies, B. Sheppard, & R. Lewicki (Eds), *Research on negotiations* (Vol. 5, pp. 219–247). Greenwich, CT: JAI Press.

Buchanan, B. (1974). Building organizational commitment: The socialization of managers in work organizations. *Administrative Science Quarterly, 19*, 533–546.

Buss, A. H. (1961). *The psychology of aggression*. New York: Wiley.

Butler, J. R., Jr. (1991). Toward understanding and measuring conditions of trust: Evolution of a conditions of trust inventory. *Journal of Management, 17*, 643–663.

Butterfield, K. D., Trevino, L. K., & Ball, G. A. (1996). Punishment from the manager's perspective: A grounded investigation and inductive model. *The Academy of Management Journal, 39*, 1479–1512.

Canning, K., & Monmarquette, C. (1991). Managerial momentum: A simultaneous model of the career progress of male and female managers. *Industrial and Labor Relations Review, 44*, 212–228.

Chiles, T. H., & McMackin, J. F. (1996). Integrating variable preferences, trust, and transaction cost economics. *Academy of Management Review, 21*, 73–99.

Citera, M., & Rentsch, J. R. (1993). Is there justice in organizational acquisitions? The role of distributive and procedural fairness in corporate acquisitions. In R. Cropanzano (Ed.), *Justice in the workplace: Approaching fairness in human resource management* (pp. 211–230). Hillsdale, NJ: Lawrence Erlbaum Associates.

Clemmer, E. C. (1993). An investigation into the relationship of fairness and customer satisfaction with services. In R. Cropanzano (Ed.), *Justice in the workplace: Approaching fairness in human resource management* (pp. 193–207). Hillsdale, NJ: Lawrence Erlbaum Associates.

Cobb, A. T., & Frey, F. M. (1996). The effects of leader fairness and pay outcomes on supervisor-subordinate relations. *Journal of Applied Social Psychology, 26*, 1401–1426.

Cobb, A. T., Wooten, K. C., & Folger, R. (1995). Justice in the making: Toward understanding the theory and practice of justice in organizational change and development. In W. A. Pasmore & R. W. Woodman (Eds.), *Research in organizational change and development* (Vol. 8, pp. 243–295). Greenwich, CT: JAI Press.

Cohen, R. L. (1982). Perceiving justice: An attributional perspective, In J. Greenberg & R. L. Cohen (Eds.), *Equity and justice in social behavior* (pp. 119–160). New York: Academic Press.

Cohen, R. L., & Greenberg, J. (1982). The justice concept in social psychology. In J. Greenberg & R. L. Cohen (Eds.), *Equity and justice in social behavior* (pp. 1–41). New York: Academic Press.

Cole, N. D., & Latham, G. G. (1997). Effects of training in procedural justice on perceptions of disciplinary fairness by unionized employees and disciplinary subject matter experts. *Journal of Applied Psychology, 82,* 699–705.

Cooper, R., & Markus, M. L. (1995). Human re-engineering. *Sloan Management Review* (Summer), 39–50.

Cowherd, D. M., & Levine, D. L. (1992). Product quality and pay equity between lower-level employees and top management: An investigation of distributive justice theory. *Administrative Science Quarterly, 37,* 302–320.

Creed, W. E., & Douglas, W.E.D. (1995). Trust in organizations: A conceptual framework linking organizational forms, managerial philosophies, and the opportunity costs of controls. In R. M. Kramer & T. R. Tyler (Eds.), *Trust in organizations: Frontiers of theory and research* (pp. 16–38). Thousand Oaks, CA: Sage Publications.

Cropanzano, R. (1993). *Justice in the workplace: Approaching fairness in human resource management.* Hillsdale, NJ: Lawrence Erlbaum Associates.

Cropanzano, R., & Folger, R. (1989). Referent cognitions and task decision autonomy: Beyond equity theory. *Journal of Applied Psychology, 74,* 293–299.

Cropanzano, R. S., Kacmar, M. K., & Bozerman, D. P. (1995). The social setting of work organizations: Politics, justice, and support. In R. Cropanzano & K. M. Kamar (Eds.), *Organizational politics, justice, and support* (pp. 1–18). Westport, CT: Quorum Books.

Cropanzano, R., & Randall, M. L. (1993). Injustice and work behavior: A historical review. In Cropanzano, R., *Justice in the workplace: Ap-*

proaching fairness in human resource management (pp. 3–20). Hillsdale, NJ: Lawrence Erlbaum Associates.

Crosby, F. (1976). A model of egoistical relative deprivation. *Psychological Review, 23,* 85–113.

Crosby, F. (1982). *Relative deprivation and working women.* New York: Oxford University Press.

Crosby, F. (1984). *Relative deprivation in organizational settings.* In L. L. Cummings & B. M. Staw (Eds.), *Research in organizational behavior* (Vol. 6, pp. 51–93). Greenwich, CT: JAI Press.

Crosby, F., & Gonzalez-Intal, M. (1984). Relative deprivation. In R. Folger (Ed.), *The sense of injustice: Social psychological perspectives* (pp. 141–166). New York: Plenum Press.

Dailey, R. C., & Delaney, J. K. (1992). Distributive and procedural justice as antecedents of job dissatisfaction and intent to turnover. *Human Relations, 45,* 305–317.

Dalton, D. R., & Todor, W. D. (1985). Gender and workplace justice: A field assessment. *Personnel Psychology, 38,* 133–151.

Daly, J. P. (1995). Explaining changes to employees: The influence of justifications and change outcomes on employees' fairness judgments. *Journal of Applied Behavioral Science, 31,* 415–428.

Daly, J. P., & Geyer, P. D. (1994). The role of fairness in implementing large-scale change: Employee evaluations of process and outcomes in seven facility relocations. *Journal of Organizational Behavior, 15,* 623–638.

Daly, J. P., & Geyer, P. D. (1995). Procedural fairness and organizational commitment under conditions of growth and decline. *Social Justice Research, 8,* 137–151.

Dasgupta, P. (1988). Trust as a commodity. In D. Gambetta (Ed.), *Trust: Making and breaking cooperative relations* (pp. 49–72). New York: Blackwell.

Davis, J. A. (1959). A formal interpretation of the theory of relative deprivation. *Sociometry, 22,* 280–296.

Deluga, R. J. (1994). Supervisor, trust building, leader-member exchange and organizational citizenship behavior. *Journal of Occupational and Organizational Psychology, 67,* 315–326.

DeMore, S. W., Fisher, J. D., & Baron, R. M. (1988). The equity-control model as a predictor of vandalism among college students. *Journal of Applied Psychology, 18,* 80–91.

Deutsch, M. (1975). Equity, equality, and need: What determines which value will be used as the basis of distributive justice? *Journal of Social Issues, 31*, 137–149.

Deutsch, M. (1985). *Distributive justice: A social psychological perspective.* New Haven: Yale University Press.

Diekman, K. A. (1997). Implicit justifications and self-serving group allocations. *Journal of Organizational Behavior, 18*, 3–16.

Dodge, A. K. (1980). Social cognition and children's aggressive behavior. *Child Development, 51*, 162–170.

Dodge, A. K., Price, J. M., Bachorowski, J., & Newman, J. P. (1990). Hostile attributional bias in severely aggressive adolescents. *Journal of Abnormal Psychology, 99*, 385–392.

Early, P. C., & Lind, E. A. (1987). Procedural justice and participation in task selection: The role of control in mediating justice judgments. *Journal of Personality and Social Psychology, 52*, 1148–1160.

Elliot, G. C., & Meeker, B. F. (1986). Achieving fairness in the face of competing concerns: The different effects of individual and group characteristics. *Journal of Personality and Social Psychology, 50*, 754–760.

Farell, D., & Rusbut, C. E. (1981). Exchange variables as predictors of job satisfaction, job commitment, and turnover: The impact of rewards, costs, alternatives, and investments. *Organizational Behavior and Human Performance, 28*, 78–95.

Farh, J. L., Podsakoff, P. M., & Organ, D. W. (1990). Accounting for organizational citizenship behavior: Leader fairness and task scope versus satisfaction. *Journal of Management, 16*, 705–721.

Festinger, L. (1954). A theory of social comparison processes. *Human Relations, 7*, 11–140.

Fine, M. (1979). Options to injustice: Seeing other lights. *Representative Research in Social Psychology, 10*, 61–76.

Folger, R. (1977). Distributive and procedural justice: Combined impact of "voice" and improvement on experienced inequity. *Journal of Personality and Social Psychology, 35*, 108–119.

Folger, R. (1986). Rethinking equity theory: A referent cognitions model. In H. W. Bierhoff, R. L. Cohen, & J. Greenberg (Eds.), *Justice in social relations* (pp. 145–162). New York: Plenum.

Folger, R. (1987). Distributive and procedural justice in the workplace. *Social Justice Research, 1*, 143–160.

Folger, R. (1993). Reactions to mistreatment at work. In J. K. Murnighan (Ed.), *Social Psychology in organizations: Advances in theory and research* (pp. 161–183). Englewood Cliffs, NJ: Prentice-Hall.

Folger, R., & Baron R. A. (1996). Violence and hostility at work: A model of reactions to perceived injustice. In G. R. Van den Bos & E. Q. Bulato (Eds.), *Workplace violence* (pp. 51–85). Washington, DC: APA.

Folger, R., & Bies, R. J. (1989). Managerial responsibilities and procedural justice. *Employee Responsibilities and Rights Journal, 2,* 79–90.

Folger, R., & Greenberg, J. (1985). Procedural justice: An interpretative analysis of personnel systems. In K. Rowland & G. Ferris (Eds.), *Research in personnel and human resources management* (Vol. 3, pp. 141–183). Greenwich, CT: JAI Press.

Folger, R., & Konovsky, M. A. (1989). Effects of procedural and distributive justice on reactions to pay raise decisions. *Academy of Management Journal, 32,* 115–130.

Folger, R., Konovsky, M. A., & Cropanzano, R. (1992). A due process metaphor for performance appraisal. In B. M. Staw & L. L. Cummings (Eds.), *Research in organizational behavior* (Vol. 14, 129–177). Greenwich, CT: JAI Press.

Folger, R., & Lewis, D. (1993). Self-appraisal and fairness in evaluation. In R. Cropanzano (Ed.), *Justice in the workplace: Approaching fairness in human resource management* (pp. 107–131). Hillsdale, NJ: Lawrence Erlbaum Associates.

Folger, R., & Martin, C. (1986). Relative deprivation and referent cognitions: Distributive and procedural justice effects. *Journal of Experimental Social Psychology, 22,* 531–546.

Folger, R., Rosenfield, D., & Robinson, T. (1983). Relative deprivation and procedural justifications. *Journal of Personality and Social Psychology, 45,* 268–273.

Friedman, R. A., & Robinson, R. J. (1993). Justice for all? Union versus management responses to unjust acts and social accounts. *The International Journal of Conflict Management, 4,* 9–117.

Fryxell, G. E., & Gordon, M. E. (1989). Workplace justice and job satisfaction as predictors with unions and management. *Academy Management Journal, 32,* 851–866.

Furby, L. (1986). Psychology and justice. In R. L. Cohen (Ed.), *Justice: Views from the social sciences* (pp. 153–203). New York: Plenum.

Giacobble-Miller, J. (1995). A test of the group values and control models of procedural justice from the competing perspective of labor and management. *Personnel Psychology, 48,* 113–142.

Gillerman, S. (1963). *Motivation and productivity.* New York: American Management Association.

Gilliland, S. W. (1993). The perceived fairness of selection systems: An organizational justice perspective. *Academy of Management Review, 18,* 694–734.

Granovetter, M. (1985). Economic action and social structure: The problem of embeddedness. *American Journal of Sociology, 91,* 481–510.

Greenberg, J. (1977). The Protestant work ethic and reactions to negative performance evaluation on a laboratory task. *Journal of Applied Psychology, 62,* 682–690.

Greenberg, J. (1978). Effects of reward value and retaliative power on allocation decisions: Justice, generosity, or greed? *Journal of Personality and Social Psychology, 36,* 367–379.

Greenberg, J. (1981). The justice of distributing scarce resources. In M. J. Lerner & S. C. Lerner (Eds.), *The justice motive in social behavior* (pp. 289–316). New York: Plenum.

Greenberg, J. (1982). Approaching equity and avoiding inequity in groups and organizations. In J. Greenberg & R. L. Cohen (Eds.), *Equity and justice in social behavior* (pp. 389–435). New York: Academic Press.

Greenberg, J. (1983). Overcoming egocentric bias in perceived fairness through self-awareness. *Social Psychology Quarterly, 46,* 152–156.

Greenberg, J. (1984). On the apocryphal nature of inequity distress. In R. Folger (Ed.), *The sense of injustice: Social psychological perspectives* (pp. 167–186). New York: Plenum.

Greenberg, J. (1986a). Determinants of perceived fairness of performance evaluations. *Journal of Applied Psychology, 71,* 340–342.

Greenberg, J. (1986b). Organizational performance appraisal procedures: What makes them fair? In R. J. Lewicki, B. H. Sheppard, & M. H. Bazerman (Eds.), *Research on negotiation in organizations* (Vol. 1, pp. 25–41). Greenwich, CT: JAI Press.

Greenberg, J. (1987a). A taxonomy of organization justice theories. *Academy of Management Review, 12,* 9–22.

Greenberg, J. (1987b). Reactions to procedural injustices in payment distributions: Do the means justify the ends? *Journal of Applied Psychology, 72,* 55–61.

Greenberg, J. (1989). Cognitive re-evaluation of outcomes in response to underpayment inequity. *Academy of Management Journal, 32,* 174–184.

Greenberg, J. (1990a). Organizational justice: Yesterday, today, and tomorrow. *Journal of Management, 16,* 399–432.

Greenberg, J. (1990b). Employee theft as a reaction to underpayment inequity: The hidden costs of pay cuts. *Journal of Applied Psychology, 75,* 561–568.

Greenberg, J. (1990c). Looking fair vs. being fair: Managing impressions of organizational justice. In L. L. Cummings & B. M. Staw (Eds.), *Research in organizational behavior* (Vol. 12, pp. 111–157). Greenwich, CT: JAI Press.

Greenberg, J. (1991). Using explanations to manage impressions of performance appraisal fairness. *Employee Responsibilities and Rights Journal, 4,* 51–60.

Greenberg, J. (1993a). The social side of fairness: Interpersonal and informal classes of organizational justice. In R. Cropanzano (Ed.), *Justice in the workplace: Approaching fairness in human resource management* (pp. 79–103). Hillsdale, NJ: Lawrence Erlbaum Associates.

Greenberg, J. (1993b). Stealing in the name of justice: Informational and interpersonal moderators of employee reactions to underpayment inequity. *Organizational Behavior and Human Decision Processes, 54,* 81–103.

Greenberg, J. (1994). Using socially fair treatment to promote acceptance of a work site smoking ban. *Journal of Applied Psychology, 79,* 288–297.

Greenberg, J. (1996). *The quest for justice: Essays and experiments.* Thousand Oaks, CA: Sage Publications.

Greenberg, J. (1997). The steal motive: Managing the social determinants of employee theft. In R. Giacalone & J. Greenberg (Eds.), *Antisocial behavior in the workplace* (pp. 85–108). Thousand Oaks, CA: Sage Publications.

Greenberg, J., & Alge, B. J. (in press). Aggressive reactions to workplace injustice. In R. W. Griffin, A. O'Leary-Kelly, & J. Collins (Eds.), *Dysfunctional behavior in organizations: Violent behaviors in organizations* (Vol. 1). Greenwich, CT: JAI Press.

Greenberg, J., & Cohen, R. L. (1982). Why justice? Normative and instrumental interpretations. In J. Greenberg & R. L. Cohen (Eds.), *Equity and justice in social behavior* (pp. 437–469). New York: Academic Press.

Greenberg, J., & Folger, R. (1983). Procedural justice, participation, and the fair process effect in groups and organizations. In P. B. Paulus (Ed.), *Basic group processes* (pp. 235–256). New York: Springer-Verlag.

Greenberg, J., & Leventhal, G. S. (1976). Equity and the use of overreward to motivate performance. *Journal of Personality and Social Psychology, 34*, 179–190.

Greenberg, J., & Scott, K. S. (1996). Why do workers bite the hands that feed them? Employee theft as a social exchange process. In L. L. Cummings & B. M. Staw (Eds.), *Research in organizational behavior* (Vol. 18, pp. 111–156). Greenwich, CT: JAI Press.

Grienberger, I. V., Rutte, C. G., & Van Knippenberg, A.F.M. (1997). Influence of social comparisons of outcomes and procedures on fairness judgments. *Journal of Applied Psychology, 82*, 913–919.

Gronroos, C. (1984). A service quality model and its marketing implications. *European Journal of Marketing, 18*, 36–44.

Grover, S. L. (1991). Predicting the perceived fairness of parental leave policies. *Journal of Applied Psychology, 76*, 247–255.

Gundykunst, W. B., & Ting-Tomey, S. (1988). Culture and affective communication. *American Behaviorist, 31*, 384–400.

Gurr, T. R. (1968). A causal model of civil strife: A comparative analysis using new indices. *American Political Science Review, 23*, 1104–1124.

Gurr, T. R. (1970). *Why men rebel.* Princeton, NJ: Princeton University Press.

Hackett, D. R., Bycio, P., & Hausdorf, P. A. (1994). Further assessments of Meyer and Allen's (1991) three-component model of organizational commitment. *Journal of Applied Psychology, 79*, 15–23.

Hardy, C. (1990). Strategy and context: Retrenchment in Canadian universities. *Organization Studies, 11*, 207–237.

Hasegawara, K. (1986). *Japanese-style management.* New York: Kondasha International.

Heilman, M. E. (1994). Affirmative action: Some unintended consequences for working women. In L. L. Cummings & B. M. Staw

(Eds.), *Research in organizational behavior* (Vol. 16, pp. 125–169). Greenwich, CT: JAI Press.

Hofstede, G. R. (1980). *Culture's consequences: International differences in work relations.* Newbury Park, CA: Sage Publications.

Hollinger, R. C., & Clark, J. P. (1983). *Theft by employees.* Lexington, MA: Lexington Books.

Homans, G. C. (1961). *Social behavior.* New York: Harcourt Brace and World.

Huseman, R. C., Hatfield, J. D., & Miles, E. W. (1987). A new perspective on equity theory: The equity sensitivity construct. *Academy of Management Review, 12,* 222–234.

Itoi, R., Obhuci, K. I., & Fukuno, M. (1996). A cross-cultural study of preference of accounts: Relationship closeness, harm severity, and motives of account making. *Journal of Applied Social Psychology, 26,* 913–934.

Jackson, L. A., Gardner, P. D., & Sullivan, L. A. (1992). Explaining gender differences in self-pay expectations: Social comparison standards and perceptions of fair pay. *Journal of Applied Psychology, 77,* 651–663.

Jackson, S. E., Stone, V. K., & Alvarez, E. B. (1992). Socialization amidst diversity: The impact of demographics on work team old-timers and newcomers. In L. L. Cummings & B. M. Staw (Eds.), *Research in organizational behavior* (Vol. 15, pp. 45–109). Greenwich, CT: JAI Press.

James, D. (1993). The social context of organizational justice: Cultural, intergroup, and structural effects on justice behaviors and perceptions. In R. Cropanzano (Ed.), *Justice in the workplace: Approaching fairness in human resource management* (pp. 21–50). Hillsdale, NJ: Lawrence Erlbaum Associates.

Jaros, S. J., Jermier, J. M., Koehler, J. W., & Sincich, T. (1993). Effects of continuance, affective, and moral commitment on the withdrawal process: An evaluation of eight structural equation models. *Academy of Management Journal, 36,* 951–995.

Jasso, G. (1977). Distributive justice and earned income. *American Sociological Review, 42,* 639–651.

Jasso, G. (1978). On the justice of earnings: A new specification of the justice evaluation function. *American Journal of Sociology, 83,* 1398–1419.

Jasso, G. (1980). A new theory of distributive justice. *American Sociological Review, 45,* 3–32.

Jasso, G. (1983). Fairness of individual rewards and fairness of the reward distribution: Specifying the inconsistency between the micro and macro principles of justice. *Social Psychology Quarterly, 46,* 185–199.

Jasso, G. (1994). Assessing individual and group differences in the sense of justice: Framework and application to gender differences in the justice of earnings. *Social Science Research, 23,* 368–406.

Johnson-George, C., & Swap, W. C. (1982). Measurement of specific interpersonal trust: Construction and validation of a scale to assess trust in a specific other. *Journal of Personality and Social Psychology, 43,* 1306–1317.

Joy, V. L., & Witt, L. A. (1992). Delay of gratification as a moderator of the procedural justice-distributive justice relationship. *Group and Organization Management, 17,* 297–308.

Kabanoff, B. (1991). Equity, equality, power, and conflict. *Academy of Management Review, 16,* 416–441.

Kahn, A., Nelson, R. E., & Gareddert, W. P. (1980). Sex of the subject and sex composition of the group as determinants of reward allocations. *Journal of Personality and Social Psychology, 38,* 737–750.

Kahn, A., O'Leary, V. E., Krulewitz, J. E., & Lamm, H. (1980). Equity and equality: Male and female means to a just end. *Basic and Applied Social Psychology, 1,* 173–197.

Kahneman, D., & Tversky, A. (1982). Availability and the simulation heuristic. In D. Kahneman, P. Slovic, & A. Tversky (Eds.), *Judgment under uncertainty: Heuristics and biases* (pp. 201–208). New York: Cambridge University Press.

Katz, D. (1960). The functional approach to the study of attitudes. *Public Opinion Quarterly, 24,* 163–204.

Katz, D., & Kahn, R. L. (1978). *The social psychology of organizations* (2nd Ed.). New York: Wiley.

Keeley, M. A. (1988). A social-justice approach to organizational evaluation. *Administrative Science Quarterly, 23,* 272–292.

Kidd, R. F., & Utne, M. K. (1978). Reactions to inequity: A prospective on the role of attributions. *Law and Human Behavior, 2,* 301–312.

Kidron, A. (1978). Work values and organizational commitment. *Academy of Management Journal, 21*, 239–247.

Kidwell, R. E., Jr., & Bennett, N. (1994). Employee reactions to electronic systems. *Group and Organization Management, 19*, 203–218.

Kim, W. C., & Mauborgne, R. A. (1995). A procedural justice model of strategic decision making: Strategy content implications in the multinational. *Organizational Science, 6*, 44–61.

Kim, W. C., & Mauborgne, R. A. (1996). Procedural justice and managers' in-role and extra-role behavior: The case of the multinationals. *Management Science, 42*, 499–515.

Kim, W. C., & Mauborgne, R. A. (1997). Fair process: Managing in the knowledge economy. *Harvard Business Review* (July–August), 65–75.

Konovsky, M. A., & Brockner, J. (1993). Managing victim and survivor layoff reactions: A procedural justice perspective. In R. Cropanzano (Ed.), *Justice in the workplace: Approaching fairness in human resource management* (pp. 133–153). Hillsdale, NJ: Lawrence Erlbaum Associates.

Konovsky, M. A., & Cropanzano, R. (1993). Justice considerations in employee drug testing. In R. Cropanzano (Ed.), Justice in the workplace: Approaching fairness in human resource management (pp. 171–192). Hillsdale, NJ: Lawrence Erlbaum Associates.

Konovsky, M. A., & Pugh, S. D. (1993). Citizenship behavior and social exchange. *Academy of Management Journal, 37*, 656–669.

Korsgaard, M. A., Schweiger, D. M., & Sapienza, H. R. (1995). Building commitment, attachment, and trust in strategic decision-making teams: The role of procedural justice. *Academy of Management Journal, 38*, 60–84.

Kozlowski, S.W.J., Chao, G. T., Smith, E. M., & Hedlund, J. (1993). Organizational downsizing: Strategies, interventions, and research implications. *International Review of Industrial and Organizational Psychology, 8*, 263–332.

Kramer, R. M. (1991). Intergroup relations and organizational dilemmas: The role of the categorization processes. In L. L. Cummings & B. M. Staw (Eds.), *Research in Organizational Behavior* (Vol. 13, pp. 191–228). Greenwich, CT: JAI Press.

Landy, F. J., Barnes, J. L., & Murphy, K. R. (1978). Correlates of perceived fairness and accuracy of performance evaluation. *Journal of Applied Psychology, 63*, 751–754.

Landy, F. J., Barnes-Farrell, J., & Cleveland, J. N. (1980). Perceived fairness and accuracy of performance evaluation. *Journal of Applied Psychology, 65,* 355–356.

Lansberg, I. (1984). Hierarchy as a mediator of fairness: A contingency approach to distributive justice in organizations. *Journal of Applied Social Psychology, 14,* 124–135.

Lawler, E. E., III. (1968). Effects of hourly overpayment on productivity and work quality. *Journal of Personality and Social Psychology, 10,* 306–313.

Lawler, E. E., III. (1971). *Pay and organizational effectiveness: A psychological view.* New York: McGraw-Hill.

Lawler, E. J., & Yoon, J. (1996). Commitment in exchange relations: Test of a theory of relational cohesion. *American Sociological Review, 61,* 89–108.

Leck, J. D., Saunders, D. M., & Charbonneau, M. (1996). Affirmative action programs: An organizational justice perspective. *Journal of Organizational Behavior, 17,* 79–89.

Lerner, M. J. (1970). The desire for justice and reactions to victims. In J. Hacaulay & L. Berkowitz (Eds.), *Altruism and helping behavior.* New York: Academic Press.

Lerner, M. J. (1975). The justice motive in social behavior. *Journal of Social Issues, 31,* 1–20.

Lerner, M. J. (1977). The justice motive: Some hypotheses as to its origins and forms. *Journal of Personality, 45,* 1–52.

Lerner, M. J. (1980). *The belief in a just world: A fundamental delusion.* New York: Plenum Press.

Lerner, M. J. (1981). The justice motive in human relations. Some thoughts on what we know and need to know about justice. In M. J. Lerner & S. C. Lerner (Eds.), *The justice motive in social behavior* (pp. 11–35). New York: Plenum Press.

Lerner, M. J. (1987). Integrating societal and psychological rules of entitlement: The basic task of each social actor and fundamental problem for the social sciences. *Social Justice Research, 1,* 107–125.

Lerner, M. J., Miller, D. T., & Holmes, J. G. (1976). Deserving and the emergence of forms of justice. In L. Berkowitz & E. Walster (Eds.), *Advances in experimental social psychology* (Vol. 9, pp. 134–162). New York: Academic Press.

Leung, K. (1987). Some determinants of reactions to procedural models for social resolution: A cross-cultural study. *Journal of Personality and Social Psychology, 53*, 898–908.

Leung, K., & Lind, A. E. (1986). Procedural justice and culture: Effects of culture, gender, and investigator status on procedural preferences. *Journal of Personality and Social Psychology, 6*, 1134–1140.

Leung, K., & Park, H. J. (1986). Effects of interactional goal on choice of allocation role: A cross-national study. *Organizational Behavior and Human Decision Processes, 37*, 111–120.

Leventhal, G. S. (1976). The distinction of rewards and resources in groups and organizations. In L. Berkowitz & E. Walster (Eds.), *Advances in experimental social psychology* (Vol. 9, pp. 91–131). New York: Academic Press.

Leventhal, G. S. (1980). What should be done with equity theory? In K. J. Gergen, M. S. Greenberg, & R. H. Willis (Eds.), *Social exchange: Advances in theory and research* (pp. 27–55). New York: Plenum.

Leventhal, G. S., Karuza, J., & Fry, W. R. (1980). Beyond fairness: A theory of allocation preferences. In G. Mikula (Ed.), *Justice and social interaction* (pp. 167–218). New York: Springer-Verlag.

Leventhal, G. S., & Lane, D. W. (1970). Sex, age, and equity behavior. *Journal of Personality and Social Psychology, 15*, 312–316.

Leventhal, G. S., Michaels, J. W., & Sanford, C. (1972). Inequity and interpersonal conflict: Reward allocation and secrecy about reward as methods of preventing conflict. *Journal of Personality and Social Psychology, 23*, 88–102.

Levin, I., & Stokes, J. P. (1989). Dispositional approach to job satisfaction: Role of negative affectivity. *Journal of Applied Psychology, 74*, 752–758.

Lind, A. E. (1995). Justice and authority in organizations. In R. Cropanzano & K. M. Kamar (Eds.), *Organizational politics, justice, and support* (pp. 83–96). Westport, CT: Quorum Books.

Lind, A. E. (1997). Litigation and claiming in organizations: Antisocial behavior or quest for justice? In R. Giacalone & J. Greenberg (Eds.), *Antisocial behavior in the workplace* (pp. 150–171). Thousand Oaks, CA: Sage Publications.

Lind, A. E., & Tyler, T. R. (1988). *The social psychology of procedural justice.* New York: Plenum.

Lind, A. E., Tyler, T. R., & Huo, Y. J. (1997). Procedural justice context and culture: Variation in the antecedents of procedural justice judgments. *Journal of Personality and Social Psychology, 73*, 767–780.

Lissak, R. J. (1983). Procedural fairness: How employees evaluate procedures. *Unpublished doctoral dissertation*. Urbana: University of Illinois.

Lyness, K. S., & Thompson, D. E. (1997). Above the glass ceiling? A comparison of matched samples of female and male executives. *Journal of Applied Psychology, 82*, 359–375.

Magner, N. R., Rahman, M., & Walker, R. B. (1996). The interactive effect of outcome favorability and procedural justice in work resource allocation on work performance. *Journal of Applied Social Psychology, 26*, 825–842.

Major, B., & Deaux, K. (1982). Individual differences in justice behavior. In J. Greenberg & R. L. Cohen (Eds.), *Equity and justice in social behavior* (pp. 43–76). New York: Academic Press.

Mann, L., Radford, M., & Kanagawa, C. (1985). Cross-cultural differences in children's use of decision rules: A comparison between Japan and Australia. *Journal of Personality and Social Psychology, 49*, 1557–1564.

Mannix, E. A., Neale, M. A., & Northcraft, G. B. (1995). Equity, equality, or need? The effects of organizational culture on the allocation of benefits and burdens. *Organizational Behavior and Human Decision Processes, 62*, 276–286.

Manogran, P., Stauffer, J., & Conlon, E. J. (1994). Leader-member exchange as a key mediating variable between employees' perceptions of fairness and organizational citizenship behavior. *Academy of Management Best Paper Proceedings*, 249–253.

Marin, G. (1981). Perceiving justice across cultures: Equity vs. equality in Colombia and the United States. *International Journal of Psychology, 16*, 153–159.

Martin, J. (1981). Relative deprivation: A theory of distributive injustice for an era of shrinking resources. In L. L. Cummings & B. M. Staw (Eds.), *Research in organizational behavior* (Vol. 3, pp. 53–107). Greenwich, CT: JAI Press.

Martin, J. (1984). Inequality, distributive justice, and organizational illegitimacy. In J. K. Murnighan (Ed.), *Social psychology in organizations: Advances in theory and research* (pp. 296–321). Englewood Cliffs, NJ: Prentice-Hall.

Martin, J., & Harder, J. W. (1987). Bread and roses: Justice and the distribution of financial and socioemotional rewards in organizations. *Social Justice Research, 7*, 241–264.

Martin, J., & Murray, A. (1984). Catalysts for collective violence: The importance of a psychological approach. In R. Folger (Ed.), *The sense of injustice: Social psychological perspectives* (pp. 95–139). New York: Plenum Press.

Mayer, R. C., Davis, J. M., & Schoorman, F. D. (1995). An integrative model of organizational trust. *Academy of Management Review, 20*, 709–734.

McAllister, D. J. (1995). Affect and cognition-based trust as foundations for interpersonal cooperation in organizations. *Academy of Management Journal, 38*, 24–59.

McFarlane-Shore, L., & Shore, T. H. (1995). Perceived organizational support and organizational justice. In R. Cropanzano & K. M. Kamar (Eds.), *Organizational politics, justice, and support* (pp. 149–164). Westport, CT: Quorum Books.

McFarlin, D. B., & Sweeney, P. D. (1992). Distributive and procedural justice as predictors of satisfaction with personal and organizational outcomes. *Academy of Management Journal, 35*, 26–637.

McFarlin, D. B., & Sweeney, P. D. (1996). Does having a say matter if you get your way? Instrumental and value-expressive effects of employee voice. *Basic and Applied Social Psychology, 18*, 289–303.

McLean-Parks, J., & Kidder, D. L. (1994). Till death do part: Changing work relationships in the 1990s. In C. L. Copper & D. M. Rousseau (Eds.), *Trends in organizational behavior* (Vol. 1, pp. 111–136). New York: Wiley.

Meindl, J. R. (1989). Managing to be fair: An exploration of values, motives, and leadership. *Administrative Science Quarterly, 343*, 252–276.

Meindl, J. R., Cheng, Y. K., & Jun, L. (1990). Distributive justice in the workplace: Preliminary data on managerial preferences in the PRC. *Research in Personnel and Human Resources Management, Supplement 2*, 221–236.

Merton, R., & Rossi, A. S. (1957). Contribution to the theory of reference group behavior. In R. Merton (Ed.), *Social theory and social structure*. New York: Free Press.

Meyer, J. P., & Allen, N. J. (1984). Testing the "side-bet theory" of organizational commitment: Some methodological considerations. *Journal of Applied Psychology, 69*, 372–378.

Meyer, J. P., & Allen, N. J. (1991). A three-component conceptualization of organizational commitment. *Human Resource Management, 1*, 61–89.

Meyer, J. P., Allen, N. J., & Smith, C. A. (1993). Commitment to organization and occupations: Extension and test of a three-component conceptualization. *Journal of Applied Psychology, 78*, 538–551.

Miceli, M. P. (1993). Justice and pay system satisfaction. In R. Cropanzano (Ed.), *Justice in the workplace: Approaching fairness in human resource management* (pp. 257–283). Hillsdale, NJ: Lawrence Erlbaum Associates.

Mikula, G. (1980). On the role of justice in allocation decisions. In G. Mikula (Ed.), *Justice and social interaction* (pp. 127–166). New York: Springer-Verlag.

Miles, E. W., Hatfield, J. D., & Huseman, R. C. (1994). Equity sensitivity and outcome importance. *Journal of Organizational Behavior, 15*, 585–596.

Mowday, R. T., Porter, L. W., & Steers, R. M. (1982). *Employee-organizational linkages: The psychology of commitment, absenteeism, and turnover.* New York: Academic Press.

Mowday, R. T., Steers, R. M., & Porter, L. W. (1979). The measurement of organizational commitment. *Journal of Vocational Behavior, 14*, 224–247.

Murphy, K. R. (1986). When your top choice turns you down: Effects of Rejected offers on utility of selection tests. *Psychological Bulletin, 99*, 133–138.

Murphy-Berman, V., Berman, J. J., Sigh, P., Pachauri, A., & Kumar, P. (1984). Factors affecting allocation to needy and meritorious recipients: A cross-cultural comparison. *Journal of Personality and Social Psychology, 46*, 1267–1272.

Neuman, J. H., & Baron, R. A. (1997). Aggression in the workplace. In R. Giacalone & J. Greenberg (Eds.), *Antisocial behavior in the workplace* (pp. 37–67). Thousand Oaks, CA: Sage Publications, Inc.

Niehoff, B. P., & Moorman, R. H. (1993). Justice as a mediator of the relationship between methods of monitoring and organizational citizenship behaviors. *Academy of Management Journal, 36*, 527–556.

Novelli, L., Jr., Kirkman, B. L., & Shapiro, D. L. (1995). Effective implementation of organizational change: An organizational justice perspective. In C. L. Cooper & D. M. Rousseau (Eds.), *Trends in organizational behavior* (Vol. 2, pp. 15–36). New York: Wiley.

O'Leary-Kelly, A. M., Griffin, R. W., & Glew, D. J. (1996). Organization-motivated aggression: A research framework. *Academy of Management Review, 21*, 225–253.

Opotow, S., & Clayton, S. (1994). Green justice: Conceptions of fairness and the natural world. *Journal of Social Issues, 50*, 1–11.

O'Reilly, C. A., III, & Puffer, S. (1989). The impact of rewards and punishments in a social context: A laboratory and field experiment. *Journal of Occupational Psychology, 62*, 41–53.

Organ, D. W. (1988). *Organizational citizenship behavior: The good soldier syndrome*. Lexington, MA: Lexington Books.

Organ, D. W. (1990). The motivational basis of organizational citizenship behavior. In B. M. Staw & L. L. Cummings (Eds.), *Research in organizational behavior* (Vol. 16, pp. 43–72). Greenwich, CT: JAI Press.

Organ, D. W., & Konovsky, M. (1989). Cognitive versus affective determinants of organizational citizenship behavior. *Journal of Applied Psychology, 74*, 157–164.

Organ, D. W., & Moorman, R. H. (1993). Fairness and organizational citizenship behavior: What are the connections? *Social Justice Research, 16*, 5–18.

Parker, C. P., Bales, B. B., & Christiansen, N. D. (1997). Support for affirmative action, justice perceptions, and work attitudes: A study of gender and racial-ethnic group differences. *Journal of Applied Psychology, 82*, 376–389.

Pfeffer, J. (1983). Organizational demography. In L. L. Cummings & B. M. Staw (Eds.), *Research in organizational behavior* (Vol. 5, pp. 299–357). Greenwich, CT: JAI Press.

Pfeffer, J., & Langton, N. (1988). Wage inequity and the organization of work: The case of academic departments. *Administrative Science Quarterly, 33*, 588–606.

Porter, L. W., Steers, R. M., Mowday, R. T., & Boulian, P. V. (1974). Organizational commitment, job satisfaction, and turnover among psychiatric technicians. *Journal of Applied Psychology, 4*, 603–609.

Price, J. L., & Mueller, C. W. (1986). *Handbook of organizational measurement*. Marshfield, MA: Pitman.

Pritchard, R. (1969). Equity theory: A review and critique. *Organizational Behavior and Human Performance, 4,* 75–94.

Randall, C. S., & Mueller, C. W. (1995). Extensions of justice theory: Justice evaluations and employees' reactions in a natural setting. *Social Psychology Quarterly, 58,* 178–194.

Rawls, J. (1971). *A theory of justice*. Cambridge, MA: Harvard University Press.

Reichers, A. (1986). Conflict and organizational commitments. *Journal of Applied Psychology, 71,* 508–514.

Reis, H. T. (1984). The multidimensionality of justice. In R. Folger (Ed.), *The sense of injustice: Social psychological perspectives* (pp. 25–61). New York: Plenum.

Rentsch, J. R., & Schneider, B. (1991). Expectations for postcombination organizational life: A study of responses to mergers and acquisitions scenarios. *Journal of Applied Social Psychology, 21,* 233–252.

Rhodebeck, L. (1981). Group deprivation: An alternative model for explaining collective political action. *Micropolitics, 1,* 239–267.

Riordan, C. M., & McFarlane Shore, L. (1997). Demographic diversity and employee attitudes: An empirical examination of relational demography within work units. *Journal of Applied Psychology, 82,* 342–358.

Robertson, I. T., & Smith, M. (1989). Personnel selection methods. In M. Smith & I. T. Robertson (Eds.), *Advances in selection assessment* (pp. 89–112). Chichester, England: Wiley and Sons.

Robinson, S. L., & Morrison, E. W. (1995). Psychological contracts and organizational citizenship behavior: The effect of unfulfilled obligations on civic virtue behavior. *Journal of Organizational Behavior, 16,* 289–298.

Ross, M., Thibaut, J. W., & Evenbeck, S. (1971). Some determinants of the intensity of social protest. *Journal of Experimental Social Psychology, 7,* 401–418.

Rousseau, D. M. (1989). Psychological and implied contracts in organizations. *Employee Rights and Responsibilities Journal, 2,* 121–139.

Rousseau, D. M. (1995). *Psychological contracts in organizations: Understanding written and unwritten agreements*. Thousand Oaks: Sage Publications.

Rubin, Z., & Peplau, L. A. (1975). Who believes in a just world? *Journal of Social Issues, 31*, 65–89.

Runciman, W. G. (1966). *Relative deprivation and social justice: A study of attitudes to social inequality in twentieth-century England*. Berkeley, CA: University of California Press.

Rutte, C. G., & Messick, D. M. (1995). An integrated model of perceived unfairness in organizations. *Social Justice Research, 3*, 239–261.

Saal, F. E., & Moore, M. S. (1993). Perceptions of promotion fairness and promotion candidates' qualifications. *Journal of Applied Psychology, 78*, 105–110.

Sapienza, H. J., & Korsgaard, M. A. (1996). Procedural justice in entrepreneur-investor relations. *Academy of Management Journal, 39*, 544–574.

Sashkin, M., & Williams, R. L.(1990). Does fairness make a difference? *Organizational Dynamics, 19*, 56–71.

Schlenker, B. R. (1980). *Impression management: The self-concept, social identity, and interpersonal relations*. Belmont, CA: Brooks/Cole.

Schnake, M. (1991). Organizational citizenship: A review, proposed model, and research. *Human Relations, 44*, 735–757.

Schuler, H. (1993). Social validity of selection situations: A concept and some empirical results. In H. Schuler, J. L. Farr, & M. Smith (Eds.), *Personnel selection and assessment: Individual and organizational perspectives* (pp. 11–26). Hillsdale, NJ: Lawrence Erlbaum Associates.

Scott, M. B., & Lyman, S. M. (1968). Accounts. *American Sociological Review, 33*, 46–62.

Shapiro, D. L. (1991). The effects of explanations on negative reactions to deceit. *Administrative Science Quarterly, 36*, 614–630.

Shapiro, D. L. (1993). Reconciling theoretical differences among procedural justice researchers by re-evaluating what it means to have one's views "considered": Implications for third-party managers. In R. Cropanzano (Ed.), *Justice in the workplace: Approaching fairness in human resource management* (pp. 51–78). Hillsdale, NJ: Lawrence Erlbaum Associates.

Shaver, K. G. (1985). *The attribution of blame: Causality, responsibility, and blameworthiness*. New York: Springer-Verlag.

Sheppard, B. H., & Lewicki, R. J. (1987). Toward general principles of managerial fairness. *Social Justice Research, 1*, 161–176.

Sheppard, B. H., Lewicki, R. J., & Minton, J. W. (1992). *Organizational justice: The search of fairness in the workplace.* New York: Lexington Books.

Sitkin, S. B., Sucliffe, K. M., & Reed, G. L. (1993). Prescriptions for justice: Using social accounts to legitimate the exercise of professional control. *Social Justice Research, 6,* 87–111.

Skarlicki, D. P., & Latham, G. (1996). Increasing citizenship behavior within a labor union: A test of organizational justice theory. *Journal of Applied Psychology, 81,* 161–169.

Smith, C. A., Organ, D. W., & Near, J. P. (1983). Organizational citizenship behavior: Its nature and antecedents. *Journal of Applied Psychology, 68,* 653–663.

Smith, H. J., Spears, R., & Oyen, M. (1994). People like us: The influence of personal deprivation and group membership salience on justice evaluations. *Journal of Experimental Social Psychology, 30,* 277–299.

Staw, B. M. (1981). The escalation of commitment to a course of action. *Academy of Management Review, 6,* 577–587.

Steensma, H., Hartigh, D. E., & Lucardie, E. (1994). Social categories, just world belief, locus of control, and causal attributions of occupational accidents. *Social Justice Research, 7,* 281–299.

Steiner, D. D., & Gilliland, S. W. (1996). Fairness reactions to personnel selection techniques in France and the United States. *Journal of Applied Psychology, 81,* 134–141.

Stepina, L. P., & Perrewe, P. L. (1991). The stability of comparative referent choice and feelings of inequity: A longitudinal field study. *Journal of Organizational Behavior, 12,* 185–200.

Stern, P. C., & Dietz, J. (1994). The value basis of environmental concern. *Journal of Social Issues, 50,* 65–84.

Stevens, T. A., Beyer, J., & Trice, H. M. (1978). Assessing personal, role, and organizational predictors of managerial commitment. *Academy of Management Journal, 21,* 380–396.

Stroesser, S. J., & Heuer, L. B. (1996). Cognitive bias in procedural justice: Formation and applications of illusory correlations in perceived intergroup fairness. *Journal of Personality and Social Psychology, 71,* 717–728.

Sugawara, I., & Huo, Y. J. (1994). Disputes in Japan: A cross-cultural test of the procedural justice model. *Social Justice Research, 7,* 129–144.

Summers, T. P., & Hendrix, W. H. (1991). Modeling the role of pay equity perceptions: A field study. *Journal of Occupational Psychology, 64*, 145–157.

Sweeney, P. D., & McFarlin, D. B. (1993). Workers' evaluations of the "ends" and the "means": An examination of four models of distributive and procedural justice. *Organizational Behavior and Human Decision Processes, 55*, 23–40.

Sweeney, P. D., & McFarlin, D. B. (1997). Process and outcome: Gender differences in the assessment of justice. *Journal of Organizational Behavior, 18*, 83–98.

Sweeney, P. D., McFarlin, D. B., & Cotton, J. L. (1991). Locus of control as a moderator of the relationship between perceived influence and procedural justice. *Human Relations, 44*, 333–342.

Taggart, J. H. (1997). Autonomy and procedural justice: A framework for evaluating subsidiary strategy. *Journal of International Business Studies, 28*, 51–76.

Tajfel, H., & Turner, J. (1979). An integrative theory of intergroup conflict. In W. G. Austin & S. Worchel (Eds.), *The social psychology of intergroup relationships* (pp. 33–47). Monterey, CA: Brooks/Cole.

Taylor, M. S., Tracy, K. B., Renard, M. K., Harrison, J. K., & Carroll, S. J. (1995). Due process in performance appraisal: A quasi-experiment in procedural justice. *Administrative Science Quarterly, 40*, 495–523.

Tedeschi, J. T., & Felson, R. B. (1994). *Violence, aggression, and coercive actions.* Washington, DC: American Psychological Association.

Tedeschi, J. T., & Reiss, M. (1981). Verbal strategies in impression management. In C. Antaki (Ed.), *The psychology of ordinary explanations of social behavior* (pp. 271–309). New York: Academic Press.

Tetlock, P. E. (1985). Toward an intuitive politician model of attribution processes. In B. R. Schlenker (Ed.), *The self and social life* (pp. 203–234). New York: McGraw-Hill.

Thibaut, J. W., & Walker, L. (1975). *Procedural justice: A psychological analysis.* Hillsdale, NJ: Lawrence Erlbaum Associates.

Thibaut, J. W., & Walker, L. (1978). A theory of procedure. *California Law Review, 66*, 541–566.

Tornblom, K. Y. (1977). Distributive justice: Typology and propositions. *Human Relations, 30*, 1–24.

Trevino, L. K. (1992). The social effects of punishment in organizations: A justice perspective. *Academy of Management Review, 47*, 647–676.

Triandis, H. C. (1989). The self and social behavior in different cultural contexts. *Psychological Review, 96*, 506–520.

Tsui, A. S., & O'Reilly, C. A., III. (1989). Beyond simple demographic effects: The importance of relational demography in superior-subordinate goals. *Academy of Management Journal, 32*, 402–423.

Tversky, A., & Kahneman, D. (1981). The framing of decisions and the psychology of choice. *Science, 211*, 453–458.

Tyler, T. R. (1987). Conditions leading to the value expressive effects in judgments of procedural justice: A test of four models. *Journal of Personality and Social Psychology, 52*, 333–344.

Tyler, T. R. (1988). What is procedural justice? Criteria used by citizens to assess the fairness of legal procedures. *Law and Society Review, 22*, 301–355.

Tyler, T. R. (1989). The psychology of procedural justice: A test of the group value model. *Journal of Personality and Social Psychology, 57*, 830–838.

Tyler, T. R. (1994). Psychological models of the justice motive: Antecedents of distributive and procedural justice. *Journal of Personality and Social Psychology, 67*, 850–863.

Tyler, T. R., & Bies, R. J. (1990). Beyond formal procedures: The interpersonal context of procedural justice. In J. S. Carroll (Ed.), *Applied social psychology and organizational settings* (pp. 77–98). Hillsdale, NJ: Lawrence Erlbaum Associates.

Tyler, T. R., & Caine, A. (1981). The influence of outcomes and procedures on satisfaction with formal leaders. *Journal of Personality and Social Psychology, 41*, 642–655.

Tyler, T. R., & Degoey, P. (1995). Trust in organizational authorities: The influence of motive attributions on willingness to accept decisions. In R. M. Kramer & T. R. Tyler (Eds.), *Trust in organizations: Frontiers of theory and research* (pp. 331–356). Thousand Oaks, CA: Sage Publications.

Tyler, T. R., Degoey, P., & Smith, H. (1996). Understanding why the justice of group procedures matters: A test of the psychological dynamics of the group-value model. *Journal of Personality and Social Psychology, 70*, 913–930.

Tyler, T. R., & Folger, R. (1980). Distributional and procedural aspects of satisfaction with citizens' police encounters. *Basic and Applied Social Psychology, 1*, 281–292.

Tyler, T. R., & Lind, E. A. (1992). A relational model of authority in groups. In M. Zanna (Ed.), *Advances in experimental social psychology* (Vol. 25, pp. 115–191). New York: Lexington Books.

Tyler, T. R., Rasinski, K., & Spodick, N. (1985). The influence of voice satisfaction with leaders: Exploring the meaning of process control. *Journal of Personality and Social Psychology, 48*, 72–81.

Ulrich, D. (1998). A new mandate for human resources. *Harvard Business Review* (January-February), 124–134.

Van den Bos, K., Vermont, R., & Wilke, A.M.H. (1997). Procedural and distributive justice: What is fair depends more on what comes first than on what comes next. *Journal of Personality and Social Psychology, 72*, 95–104.

Van Yperen, N. W., Hagedoorn, M. & Geurts, S.A.E. (1996). Intent to leave and absenteeism as reactions to perceived inequity: The role of psychological and social constraints. *Journal of Occupational and Organizational Psychology, 69*, 367–372.

Von Bettalanffy, L. (1962). General system theory: A critical review. *General Systems, 7*, 1–20.

Walsh, J. P. (1988). Top management turnover following mergers and acquisitions. *Strategic Management Journal, 9*, 173–183.

Walster, E.G.W., Walster, G. W., & Berscheid, E. (1976). New directions in equity research. In L. Berkowitz (Ed.), *Advances in experimental social psychology* (Vol. 9, pp. 1–43). New York: Academic Press.

Walster, E.G.W., Walster, G. W., & Berscheid, E. (1978). *Equity: Theory and research*. Boston: Allyn and Bacon.

Watson, D., & Clark, L. A. (1984). Negative affectivity: The disposition to experience aversive emotional states. *Psychological Bulletin, 96*, 465–490.

Watson, D., Clark, L. A., & Tellegen, A. (1988). Development and validation of brief measures of positive and negative affect: The PANAS scales. *Journal of Personality and Social Psychology, 54*, 1063–1070.

Weick, W. E. (1966). The concept of equity in the perception of pay. *Administrative Science Quarterly, 11*, 414–439.

Wesolowski, M. A., & Mossholder, K. M. (1997). Relational demography in supervisor-subordinate dyads: Impact on subordinate job satisfaction, burnout, and perceived procedural justice. *Journal of Organizational Behavior, 18*, 351–362.

Wright, S. C., Taylor, D. M., & Moghaddam, F. M. (1990). Responding to membership in a disadvantaged group: From acceptance to collective protest. *Journal of Personality and Social Psychology, 23*, 301–310.

Zand, D. E. (1972). Trust and managerial problem solving. *Administrative Science Quarterly, 17*, 229–239.

Zeffane, R. (1994). Patterns of organizational commitment and perceived management style: A comparison of public and private sector employees. *Human Relations, 47*, 977–1010.

Zucker, L. G. (1986). Production of trust: Institutional sources of economic structure, 1840–1920. In L. L. Cummings & B. M. Staw (Eds.), *Research in organizational behavior* (Vol. 8, pp. 53–111). Greenwich, CT: JAI Press.

Index

About the Author

CONSTANT D. BEUGRÉ is Assistant Professor of Management at Kent State University. Dr. Beugré has been a Research Associate at Rensselaer Polytechnic Institute, Lally School of Management and Technology and a Research Analyst at the Research Foundation for Mental Hygiene in Albany, New York. He has also taught at the National University of the Ivory Coast, West Africa.